Blindsided by Addiction

Blindsided by Addiction:

The Science of the Loss of Self-Control

Arthur Tomie, PhD

Rutgers University

ZT Enterprises, LLC

Library of Congress Cataloging-in-Publication Data

Arthur Tomie, 1946-

Blindsided by Addiction /

By Arthur Tomie. Includes Preface, Introduction, Bibliography, Appendix, Glossary.

ISBN-13: 9798667169802

Table of Contents

Preface

This book is about drug addiction. This book describes, from the perspective of an experimental laboratory addiction research scientist, the early stages of the process of becoming addicted. This book speaks to those who are beginning to experiment with drug use, and, is particularly relevant for recreational drug users, too many of whom will inadvertently fall into the habit of using regularly and end up drug addicted. The intention of this book is to steer these recreational drug users clear of the "stumble" that leads the naïve and unwary among them to slip and fall into drug addiction. Specifically, this book is intended for those recreational drug users who enjoy getting high, every now and then, especially at the beginning, and then, as time goes on, getting high more and more often, with increasing frequency as drug-taking gradually becomes more a matter of routine … more automatic and habitual.

This book is intended to help those who are somewhat concerned about losing their grip, but, have not yet slowed down. This is because they have also deluded themselves into accepting the cherished fantasy that they can quit their drug use anytime they decide to do so. They are in the process of losing control of their drug-taking, but they fail to see it. This leads them to make a horrible mistake. Their drug-taking is changing. It is no longer always voluntary and decision-based. Sometimes, their drug-taking is triggered and automatically performed even when not intended, but, by default, they misconstrue these acts of drug-taking, seeing them as voluntary and intended … the same as before. This is the stumble. They continue down the garden path, on their merry way, completely unconcerned, changing nothing, except further strengthening automatic, reflexive, and unintended acts of drug-taking. Eventually, inevitably, they go too far for too long. They lose their balance. They fall over the edge, tumbling into the pit of drug addiction.

Many addicts complain that they feel victimized. They feel cheated. The horrible consequences of becoming addicted warranted a clearer and more explicit warning. They feel that they were blindsided. They never imagined that they could decide to quit drugs only to find that their decision to quit was meaningless. They never saw addiction coming for them. They never saw their acts of drug-taking as reflexive and involuntary. And, they ask, how can I put a stop to my reflexive and involuntary acts of drug-taking, that I cannot control and cannot see? That is precisely the point of this book. Don't go there. Your best defense against addiction is to stop addiction before it starts, by learning about the factors that contribute to the loss of self-control of drug-taking, and learning to spot the early signs indicating that your control of your drug-taking is slipping away.

I tried to write *Blindsided by Addiction* so that it would be accessible to the general public, to readers not trained in science or versed in scientific jargon. At the same time, I tried not to dilute the science, while making a book that is readable and enjoyable for lay persons, addiction counselors, and scientists alike. The views presented in this book are those of a basic science researcher with an abiding and long-standing interest in the etiology or origins of involuntary reflexive actions, such as the habitual drug-taking of the drug addict.

My scientific training in the study of behavior began decades ago, as a graduate student, in the human learning laboratory of Professor James Erickson at the University of Colorado. My graduate school training was interrupted in 1968, when I was drafted into military service. At Fort Ord, CA I completed Basic Training and Advanced Individual (Infantry) Training, and then I was deployed to Vietnam. From 1969-1970, I served in the Vietnam War with the 5th Infantry Division, stationed in Quang Tri Province, and operating just south of the Demilitarized Zone (DMZ). I received weapons certifications as

Sharpshooter (Machine Gun), Sharpshooter (Rifle), and Marksman (Automatic Rifle). I could not hit any targets at any distance with the .45 caliber automatic pistol. I attained the rank of Sergeant (E-5) and was awarded the Bronze Star Medal and the Army Commendation Medal, as well as various unit citations and campaign participation medals.

While serving in Vietnam, I observed widespread daily abuse of alcohol and marijuana. The marijuana, I later learned, was likely laced with opium (see Chapter 18) and was provided to US military personnel by the South Vietnamese villagers, who bartered bags of their dope for packs of American cigarettes or the cans of fruit cocktail that came with our field rations. The presence and widespread use of marijuana was nothing new to me. I grew up in East Los Angeles, near the Maravilla Housing Project, adjacent to Belvedere Park. It was not unusual to observe marijuana use, off school grounds, by Junior High School students. Marijuana use in East Los Angeles and in South Vietnam was not legal. For US military personnel, it was done on the sly, with friends, and away from the authorities, who generally looked the other way. After serving in Vietnam for a year and a day, I was honorably discharged from active duty and returned to civilian life in the United States.

I returned to graduate school with the specific intention of learning more about the scientific study of becoming addicted. While I found numerous published studies that compared addiction treatment outcomes in human subjects, I was interested in what caused addiction to develop, in the first place. I found no published experimental reports investigating the factors responsible for the emergence or development of drug addiction in humans. This area of study, the experimental analysis of the origins of addictive behaviors, was only addressed by developing an animal model of the clinical psychopathology.

Accordingly, my formal scientific training in the study of addictive behavior began in the Pavlovian conditioning laboratory of Professor David Thomas at the University of Colorado. Here we applied, in laboratory animals, the scientific experimental method, to study a relatively novel Pavlovian conditioning phenomenon, formerly called "autoshaping", now called "sign-tracking". With my associates, notably Robert Welker, Larry Engberg, Kim Wheatley, Charles Hickis, Raymond Jackson, and Greg Davitt, we noted the puzzling and curious effects of a visually localized reward signal on the subject's repetitive and reflexive performance of directed motor responding. The striking resemblance of sign-tracking behavior in the laboratory to the drug-taking actions of humans in East Los Angeles or in South Vietnam did not escape my notice. I was fascinated by sign-tracking and published my doctoral dissertation on the topic in *Science*, the flagship journal of the American Association for the Advancement of Science.

Upon joining the faculty of the Department of Psychology at Rutgers University, I set up my research lab to further my explorations of sign-tracking. My basic research studies were generously supported by grant awards from the National Science Foundation (NSF) and the National Institutes of Health (NIH). I particularly appreciate the support, guidance, and opportunity to collaborate with Professor Michael D'Amato. His wide breadth of knowledge, boundless energy, and keen sense of scientific objectivity were always evident during our daily discussions and chats. Numerous students contributed to this research, including Laura Peoples, Arthur Murphy, Bruce Lombardi, Tom Peterson, Erik Loukas, Penny Schultz, Elizabeth Towner, Regina Carelli, John Kruse, Susan Dell'Aglio, Mark Hayden, Debbie Biehl, Stephen Fath, Ines Rhor-Stafford, Steven Leichter, and Patricia Khouri.

In the early 1990's, with an eye toward further developing the application of sign-tracking to drug addiction, I began the process of moving my research laboratory to the Center of Alcohol Studies. As noted earlier, in many respects, sign-tracking in animals is mindful of the behavior of the drug addict, and this suspicion was confirmed when, at the Center of Alcohol Studies, we repeated our sign-tracking experiments in laboratory animals, while using drugs, mainly alcohol solutions, rather than food as the rewarding stimulus. Many of these studies were supported by grants awarded by the National Institutes of Health (NIH) and the National Institutes on Alcohol Abuse and Alcoholism (NIAAA). In studies conducted in collaboration with Larissa Pohorecky, Daniel Benjamin, Patricia Patterson-Buckendahl, Erich Labouvie, and Lei Yu, we observed significantly elevated levels of drug intake that were induced by sign-tracking arrangements, supporting several of the basic core predictions of the Sign-Tracking Model

Students from many different academic backgrounds made their way to the Center of Alcohol Studies to work on experiments evaluating the application of sign-tracking to drug addiction. These students include, in roughly chronological order, Jason Poco, Parth Vyas, Mitul Patel, Amit Chaudhari, Eva Mosakowski, Sneha Ganguly, Nicole Quartarolo, Devan Murphy, Carlos Cunha, Allison Aguado, Jason Di Poce, Christopher DeRenzo, Ibtesam Sabir, Beniam Biftu, Yuval Silberman, Kayon Williams, Dennis Sparta, Jeneen Interlandi, Alise Mynko, Karlvin Wong, Christine Apor, Eugene Festa, Dhagash Mehta, Amy

Janes, Christopher Franz, Brennan Thompson, Cindy Acon-Chen, Jillian Uveges, Kelly Burger, Aidaluz Tirado, Kimberly Salomon, Lauren Wong, Walaa Mohamed, Vikash Budhan, Melissa Wolff, Jason Young, Jennifer Gittleman, Erik Dranoff, Reka Hosszu, Rachel Rosenberg, William Miller, Jodi Curiotto, Kandia Lewis, Kathryn Grimes, Nick Costea, Alyssa DeFuria, Heather Jones, Sara Edwards, Colin Adams, Michelle Lincks, Shiri Nawrocki, Steffi Nadarajah, Idu Azogu, Shreyas Jaganmohan, Alec Waksman, Nikyta Sharma, Linda Farag, Olivia Harry, Kelsey Hohner, Maryam Shanehsaz, Jenna Ierley, Maryann Fakeh, Sarah Ibrahim, Tishawanie James, Michael Soliman, Mary Nashed, Alyssa Somohano, Alam Merchant, Jessica Rutyna, Nashwa Badawy, Karen Fahim, Isabel Fleury, Sureet Batth, Pamela Molina, Rita Farag, Alok Shroff, Nicole Girgis, George Eskander, Dana Sprung, Allison Samuel, Yael Malul, Karen Kwiatek, Julie Iannaccone, Racher Pan, Anna Coffman, Stephanie Liem, Kris Szalc, Emily Kaufman, Peter Jeffers, Emily Levitch, Eric Muller, Julia DiGiorgio, Collin Brown, Jenna Smego, Paul Kazelis, Ayon Iwasaki, Dimpal Kasabwala, Justyna Nagorska, Madison Surian, Jessica Rallo, and Arielle Kopp.

I am also indebted to many scientists, educators, public health officials, law enforcement officers, and drug abuse counselors for their useful advice and their support of the ideas expressed in this book. These include Terry Robinson, Roy Wise, Stanley Weiss, Rawle Gaskin, Kelli Simonetti, John Gibbon, Herb Jenkins, Shepard Siegel, Steve Maier, Charles Flaherty, Donald Hallcom, David Kearns, Jack Sherman, Rebecca Alfaro, Sid Auerbach, Eric Olsen, Shelly Flagel, Erika Witkowski, Mark Lamar, John Brogan, Stephen Bender, George Koob, Carolyn Rovee-Collier, Michael Hill, Bonnie Nolan, Skip Spear, Denise Hein, John Pearce, Noelle Jensen, Tom Discafani, John Falk, Jessica Smedley, Rob Pandina, Peter Yeager, Chip Meara, Bryan Adams, Lyra Stein, Maurice Elias, Howard Becker, Marsha Bates, Keith Murphy, Robert White, Chris Saponara, Melissa Pitman, Joseph Coronato, Stacey Milanovich-Paulis, Frank Greenagle, Peter Balsam, Frank Cimato, Jonathan Morrow, Ralph Miller, Mitchell Delmar, Donna Zaleski, Randy Gallistel, Kathleen Shoemaker, Mark Versalla, Roulla Castanos-Beaton, Bonnie Kole, Nancy Foss, Mark West, Peter McClelland, Donald Parker, David Roe, Dennis Romero, Beth Brody, Charles Sumners, and Barbara Sprechman.

To deliver the drug addiction message to a younger audience, I worked collaboratively with my wife, creative writer Barbara Zito (Tomie) and artist/illustrator Steven A. Petruccio, to produce the three illustrated scientific short stories of *The Sign Tracker Trilogy* (see Appendix). In addition, the stellar technical assistance of Kelli Curiotto, Nikyta Sharma, and Vincent Tomie were immensely helpful in producing the published paperback books and e-books, and developing the educational website (www.tailoftheraccoon.com). A second creative team developed a series of YouTube videos related to the short stories. For their endeavors, I give special thanks to illustrator/editor Jayson Gotera, audio technician David Verdini, and voice artists Ruth Sulitzer, Daniel Tims, and Victoria Tims.

Basic research scientists, from the isolation of their research laboratories, write many promissory notes, claiming that the scientific findings uncovered by their rigorously controlled experiments performed on laboratory animals will provide insights into the origins and causes of problems and disorders suffered by humans. In conjunction with my collaborators, our sign-tracking experiments begin to deliver on this promise by bringing into focus a unique and unforeseen perspective on the root cause of the loss of self-control that underlies the progression into drug addiction. To place the significance of this contribution in a broader context, it should be noted that due to a myriad of legal and ethical considerations, and despite the central importance of the problem, rigorous experimental analysis of the environmental factors that fuel the progression into drug addiction, is simply not addressable by researchers employing human subjects.

To therapists and counselors providing treatment services to individuals suffering from substance use disorder, I must explain, though not apologize, for the use of possibly derogatory and pejorative terms with respect to their clients. I carefully weighed the possibly damaging effect of terms such as "drug addict" and "drug addiction", and while not wishing to stigmatize them further, I have found that my younger audiences were confused by the terms "substance use disorder" and "individual suffering from a substance use disorder". I found that their confusion was quickly alleviated by continuing the talk using the terms "drug addiction" and "drug addict". In writing this book, my prevailing and overriding objective was to communicate most effectively with the broadest possible audience of recreational drug users, many of whom are young people in the early stages of initiating drug use. With that in mind, perhaps the desire to minimize any confusion on their part is extenuating.

My wife, Barbara Zito (Tomie), has collaborated with me on the writing of several scientific papers on sign-tracking. She has also taken the lead as creative writer and storyteller to orchestrate the production of three beautifully illustrated scientific short stories, each designed to deliver a part of the sign-tracking lesson to younger audiences. Her support, inspiration, and guidance over the years during which *Blindsided by Addiction* was written are appreciated more deeply than I can say. Our three children, Veronica, Olivia and Vincent, have contributed immensely to the appeal and pleasure of attempting this work, due, in no small part, to our meanderings in the inter-generational chasm.

Arthur Tomie

June 30, 2020

Introduction

Have you noticed that when speaking about addiction, many of us tend to make excuses for the addict? This is revealed when we say things like, "He was ensnared by addiction." To say it like this may be true, at least in some sense, but saying it in this way tends to cast the addict as hapless victim rather than as sole perpetrator. We tend to absolve the addict of blame when we describe their problem as, "… falling into addiction." But, to say "falling" suggests that the addict was, perhaps a bit careless, and then merely tripped. "Falling into addiction" implies that becoming addicted to a drug is something that just happens to you. That becoming a drug addict is as simple and effortless as losing your balance and falling over. In other words, to become addicted, you do not have to do anything, except of course, allow it to happen. When we speak about addiction, it is quite clear, based upon our choice of words, that we are accepting that addiction is not something that we do, as much as it is something that happens to us.

Do not let addiction happen to you. You can better defend yourself against becoming addicted by improving your understanding of how drug addiction sneaks up on you. The title of this book, *"Blindsided by Addiction"*, speaks to the fate of countless addicts who lost their way and then fell into the pit of addiction. They were blindsided. They never intended to become a drug addict. They never imagined that they could decide to quit and then not be able to do so. The ideas presented in this book are intended to prevent you from making the same mistake ... to keep you from blindly stumbling and then falling into addiction.

Why are we so blind to what is happening to us, as addiction closes in? Unfortunately, when it comes to addiction, we are mind-locked, by our over-blown self-confidence, by cognitive bias and momentum, and neophobia, so that we are encouraged to believe that we are in control of our drug-taking, even when we are not. This is the stumble. This is when we fall for the illusion that we are in control of our drug-taking, when we plan around the fantasy that we can quit using drugs whenever we decide to do it. Do not allow yourself to be blindsided by addiction. Do not trust in the illusion that you have complete control of your drug use. Do not allow yourself to stagger and stumble along, until you slip and fall into the pit of addiction. To avoid the stumble, learn about the fascinating science of sign-tracking and the origins of the loss of self-control. Reading this book will forever change what you are able to see as you watch yourself reach out to take the drug.

Chapter 1: The Drug Addiction Process

Have you ever watched someone you know turn into a drug addict? It's not that unusual. Certainly, not anymore. Unfortunately, with the way things are today, most of us have suffered the tragic loss of either a loved one, or a friend, or a long-time acquaintance, to the scourge of drug or alcohol addiction. In thinking for a moment about how it happened, about the sequence of events, the process of becoming addicted, were you concerned when you saw their drug-taking escalate, as they used more and more? And, then as the noose tightened, as they stumbled and began to slide, did you watch as they struggled to hang on, but lost their grip? And, were you horrified to see them surrender, falling head-long into the dark oblivion of full-blown drug addiction?

Drug addiction is an enigma. Drug addiction is difficult to understand. Particularly puzzling, and at the very heart of the matter, is the question, "How does drug addiction happen, to begin with, in the first place?" By that I mean, no one sets out to become a drug addict. No one sets out intending to lose their life to drugs. Using drugs begins voluntarily, but somehow, through repetition and ritual, drug-taking becomes unstoppable. The most obvious characteristic of addiction is that drug use seems to take on a life of its own, but how and why this happens remains largely a mystery.

The voices of addicts only serve to deepen the mystery. Many addicts tell us that their drug use escalated, even as they were trying very hard to keep it under control. Despite repeated failed attempts to maintain self-control, when addiction closed in, they were stunned, because all along they were certain that they could quit the drug if they really wanted to. They believed that quitting was just a matter of firmly deciding to do it. There is something mysterious and stealthy about the drug addiction process that allows addiction to prey upon the unsuspecting ... to victimize the innocent, those who were admittedly, and perhaps a bit foolishly, but without poor intentions, only looking to have a good time, and just for a while, every now and then. And, their risk of becoming addicted? According to them, "Not a chance, ... that will never happen to me". After all, the horrible existence of the drug addict is hardly a secret. It is well-known to everyone and has never been intended by anyone. Nevertheless, becoming addicted happens with such alarming frequency that we now find ourselves facing a full-blown, raging, out-of-control, drug addiction epidemic. But, wait a minute ... that makes no sense. I thought we all agreed that no one sets out to become a drug addict.

Apparently, somehow, through repetition and ritual, what starts out as the well-controlled, decision-based, voluntary and specifically intended drug-taking of the social, recreational drug user, mysteriously turns into the excessive, poorly managed, and out-of-control drug-taking of the drug abuser (Corbit & Janak, 2016; Everitt & Robbins, 2005; Tiffany, 1990). The loss of self-control of drug-taking is revealed by the drug abuser's lack of restraint … their inability to put an end to an ongoing drug-taking episode. Bouts and binges of uncontrollable and excessive drug-taking set the stage for the downward spiral into full-blown drug addiction. How and why drug-taking slips out of control is the perplexing mystery of drug addiction that rightfully concerns us all, and this is at the very core of the issue that must be addressed, if we are to have any hope of stemming the threat of this rising tide.

Chapter 2: Life in the Age of Addiction

The newspaper headline announced in bold letters, "Life in the Age of Addiction". It was another, in an endless stream of print stories, about the tens of thousands of Americans who, during the past year, lost their lives to drug addiction. The takeaway message is clear. The threat of addiction has never been greater than it is right now. Today we find ourselves surrounded by the opportunity to lose our way and succumb to the temptation of drugs ... to lose ourselves to addiction. Drug dealers are everywhere. They have invaded our neighborhoods, hijacked our favorite digital mass media platforms, and corrupted our pharmaceutical delivery services. Their cafeterias are open 24/7 to offer us the broadest and deepest menus of the newest branded concoctions of the most highly addictive compounds. And all of this is right there, directly in front of us, looking at us, easily within reach, literally at our fingertips. The internet and Uber now provide the ultimate in convenience ... same day delivery of our drug of choice, directly to our front door.

Blizzards of clever pitch lines unleash the inevitable avalanche, wave after wave of disturbing news cycles, each proclaiming yet another drug addiction epidemic, or worse yet, a new cluster of drug overdose deaths. And, with each cycle, the victims are younger and more widely dispersed into every urban, suburban, and rural setting than ever before. We are conscripts ... captive to the stark reality that we had never imagined or conjured up in our darkest dystopian fantasies.

All of us, regardless of where we live, are now fully aware of the daily temptation of drugs. Has it ever been easier to throw in the towel? Driven by hopelessness and despair, when have so many, given up the struggle ... seeking blissful refuge in the comfort of drug-induced oblivion? We did not ask for this, but we have no choice. This is the reality of our situation ... the reality of life in the age of addiction.

The Looming Threat:

The looming threat of addiction is always close at hand. What are we suppose to do? Remaining passive, sitting on the sidelines, while hoping for the best, no longer seems like a sensible alternative. But, then again, what is the point of recoiling in horror, deeply disturbed, paralyzed, while watching the circling of the drain? Isn't fearful inaction precisely what got us into this mess? To deal with this addiction crisis, we must change. Change is required because our current approaches to this problem are obviously not working. We have an ongoing addiction epidemic. What is the ongoing addiction epidemic telling us? It is telling us that something fundamental and crucial about addiction is not at all understood.

It is now more important than ever before, for each of us to acquire a better and deeper understanding of the process of becoming addicted. The drug addict wrecked their life by taking drugs excessively, by abusing drugs, and doing so over prolonged periods of time. The question is, "How did this happen?" According to the drug addict, the reason they chronically used the drug to excess was because they liked the feeling of getting high, which they much preferred to their normal sober state. So, they took the drug again and again, presumably each time with the intention of getting high. But, there is much more to it, beyond the mere intention of getting high, because drug abusers across the board, and irrespective of their drug of choice, will also say that their drug-taking eventually became a matter of routine, a well-learned habit, performed automatically, with little or no conscious awareness of doing it.

For example, a cocaine abuser complained of overdoing it, hitting his stash again and again, even though he could not feel any additional effect of doing more lines of cocaine. Blackout drinking from overdoing alcohol points to the same sort of thing ... automatic, involuntary, unintended hits, one after another, that appear unrelated to any observable incremental sense of pleasure derived from the alcohol-induced high. Thus, excessive drug-taking is not merely about getting high, though that is the way the drug abuser sees it. Their point of view on the matter is telling, as it says much about their limited understanding of their drug-taking, which, we believe, is what led them into eventually becoming addicted.

Our premise is that the root cause of drug addiction is the loss of control of drug-taking. From this perspective, to address the drug addiction crisis, we must get a better handle on what it is that causes control of drug-taking to slip away. In our view, the key distinction between the casual drug user and the drug abuser, who is a drug addict in training, is their ability to control their drug-taking. The casual drug user has strict control of their drug-taking. Their drug-taking is entirely voluntary. They take the drug when they decide to, and they refrain when they decide not to. The problem arises when drug-taking escapes self-control. This happens when the drug is taken even though you did not intend to do it. If you take the drug and you did not intend to do it, this drug-taking is not voluntary. This drug-taking is involuntary, and this is the root cause of the problem.

To better understand the process of becoming addicted, we need to improve our knowledge of what causes involuntary acts of drug-taking. Scientist are learning that acts of involuntary drug-taking may be triggered by the firing of brain cells located deep in the midbrain, an ancient part of the brain, filled with primitive survival reflexes. Voluntary and intended acts of drug-taking, on the other hand, come from the more recently evolved prefrontal cortex, where higher-order cognitive and executive decision-making functions reside (see Chapter 7). A key part of the problem is that automatic and reflexive and involuntary acts of drug-taking closely resemble acts of drug-taking that are voluntary and intended. This resemblance allows involuntary drug-taking to be readily mistaken for and accepted as intended and voluntary. In this way, involuntary drug-taking acts are misconstrued and erroneously processed as intended actions, which are controllable. This problem of mistaken identity allows the problem of involuntary drug-taking to fester and feed upon itself, eventually turning into the unstoppable surge we call addiction.

The problem is the undetected emergence of involuntary drug-taking that resembles and passes for voluntary drug-taking. The challenge is to identify the characteristics of involuntary drug-taking that allow you to distinguish it from voluntary drug-taking. This is what you need to know in order to recognize when addiction is coming for you … when addiction is knocking at your door. Reading this book will allow you to adjust your sights, fine tune your vigilance, to enhance what you are able to see, as you self-examine your own drug-taking behavior. The key to avoiding addiction is to become more aware of the earliest signs of involuntary drug-taking … of oncoming addiction, and to understand how those early signs, that forewarn you of incipient addiction, are camouflaged to creep on you undetected, so that you remain unalarmed. The goal, therefore, is to sharpen your acuity, to increase the likelihood that you will detect, at the earliest possible moment, the warning signs that you are losing control of your drug-taking … to stop you from becoming addicted.

Misguided Intuition:

Improving your ability to spot the earliest sign of becoming addicted is the key, because as it is, you are almost certain to miss it. The problem stems from your reliance on your gut-level intuition, which is based upon fundamentally flawed erroneous misconceptions about your ability to control the performance of your drug-taking actions (see Chapter 17). Frankly, when it comes to addiction, relying on our intuition to guide us is largely what has steered us into this mess. A widely held, "common-sense", prevailing, long-standing, and intuitive point of view is that drug addiction is self-victimization by the making of poor choices. According to this view, the drug addict is the victim of their own behavior. After all, it was they who performed the action of taking the drug. No one forced them to do it. They did this to themselves. This view is largely based on our collective intuition and our instinctive understanding of what we are seeing when the drug is self-administered. It is obvious to all that the act of drug-taking occurs because the user decided to do it. In other words, drug-taking is a voluntary response that simply reflects the individual's specific intention to self-administer the drug. While it is certainly true that this may very often be the case, it is not necessarily always the case. And this is precisely why a more inclusive and more expansive view of drug-taking is required.

Crucial to the understanding of drug addiction, and contrary to our intuition, acts of drug-taking are sometimes performed automatically and reflexively, even though the user did not intend to do it. These unintended and automatic acts of involuntary drug-taking are reflexive actions triggered by activity deep within our brain (see Chapter 7). And, as addiction takes hold, automatic and reflexive acts of drug-taking will take place with greater and greater frequency. The purpose of this book is to clue you in, so you are more vigilant and likely to detect the earliest beginnings of automatic and reflexive and involuntary acts of drug-taking.

Drug addiction is not sudden. It does not happen in an instant. Becoming addicted is a step-by-step process. Before they lost their way, before they became addicted, drug addicts were warned. They experienced the signs that their drug-taking was becoming a problem, that their drug-taking was not being properly managed, but they failed to correctly process the warning signs. They either ignored or, more likely, they misconstrued the evidence that was laid out in front of them, and they did this, not because they are self-destructive, but rather, because they were relying on their intuition to guide them, which turned out to be a big mistake. Their intuition told them that they were in control of their drug-taking when, in fact, they were not.

Addiction researchers have long noted that repeated use of the drug sets the stage for the gradual progression from voluntary and intended drug use into a form of drug-taking that is more reflexive and poorly-controlled (Corbit & Janak, 2016; deWit et al., 2012; Jellinek, 1960; Robinson & Berridge, 1993, 2001; Tiffany, 1990; Tomie, 1995, 1996). To gain a better understanding of how repeated acts of voluntary and intended drug-taking eventually lead to the development of a more automatic and reflexive form of involuntary drug-taking, we must shift our focus away from the addict, because the drug addict comes into the picture much later, at the end of the story. The drug addict is only featured after the fact, *ex-post facto*, after addiction has already taken hold. Instead, to better understand the process that eventually leads to the appearance of the drug addict, we must focus our attention on the beginning of the story. This is when following repetitions of drug-taking, acts of voluntary drug-taking begin to mutate, evolving into acts of drug-taking that are disconnected from the user's intention and awareness.

Chapter 3: In the Beginning

The addiction story begins shortly after drug use has been initiated, but before poorly controlled, unintended, and involuntary drug-taking has set in. This is when the drug's effects were still fresh and delicious, and wonderfully euphoric. For many drug addicts, this is fondly recalled as the sweet spot, as the best of times (Lewis, 2019).

Voluntary Drug-Taking:

There is a resounding chorus of agreement among drug users, and regardless of their specific drug of choice, that at least in the beginning, when they had recently started to use the drug, taking the drug only happened after they deliberately considered whether or not they should do it. It was only after giving it some thought that they would then decide to go ahead and self-administer the drug. Put another way, in the beginning, the act of drug-taking required the formation of the specific intention to do it. Clearly, each act of drug-taking was strictly a voluntary response. Each act of drug-taking was strictly decision-based and explicitly intended. This is voluntary drug use. Voluntary drug use is when drug-taking is strictly controlled, well-managed, and certainly not an everyday, habitual, or automatic sort of thing. And, this applies even for those individuals who will eventually succumb to addiction. In other words, individuals who will later eventually become addicted did not start off immediately behaving like an out-of-control drug addict.

There is widespread agreement that, in the beginning, the drug is not taken unless the user decides to do it, and, in addition, when the decision to take the drug has been made, the user is fully aware of having decided to do it. This is voluntary, decision-based, intended, controlled drug-taking, and, it should be noted, this is the form of drug-taking that is widely practiced, at least in the beginning, by virtually everyone and by anyone who has ever used a drug.

This is the voluntary drug-taking that is widely practiced by most of the general population of casual, recreational drug users, who use the drug on occasions, but not on an everyday or habitual basis. Most of these individuals will never move on to become addicted. The picture that emerges, therefore, is that in the beginning, the drug is taken only when and only if the user decides to do it, and, in addition, the user is explicitly and consciously aware of the decision to do it.

Declining the Drug:

Deciding to take the drug is one thing. Deciding not to take the drug is another. The ability of the user to refrain, the ability of the user to enforce their decision to not take the drug ... this is the single most salient and defining characteristic of voluntary drug use. Simply put, if the user decides not to take the drug, then the drug is not taken. Period. For drug use to be under strict voluntary control, the user must be able to apply the brakes, to stop an ongoing drug-taking episode. Which means that the drug is never taken automatically, and drug-taking is never reflexively triggered by any situation or circumstance, including the presence of the drug itself or the presence of drug-associated stimuli, such as the people, places, or things that were present when the drug was previously taken. In other words, the user is in control of their drug-taking if the act of drug-taking occurs only when explicitly intended, and the act of drug-taking does not occur when the intention is to refrain. This is voluntary and controlled drug-taking, and this is universally how it is, at least in the beginning.

Chapter 4: Repetition and Ritual

The next step in the drug addiction process occurs after the user has tried the drug, and experienced the drug's effects, and then the user is in the process of deciding whether to take the drug again … deciding whether to repeat the act of drug-taking. There is no such thing as a drug that is universally liked by everyone. Reactions to a drug's effects are idiosyncratic, varying greatly from one individual to the next. Not everyone who tries a drug is pleased by their reactions to the drug's effects. If you did not enjoy the drug's effects, if taking the drug made you feel anxious, or nervous, or sad, or depressed, or tired or stressed-out, then you will probably decide that this drug is not right for you, and you will probably decide not to take the drug again. Your chances of becoming addicted to this drug, whose effects were unpleasant, are quite low.

On the other hand, perhaps you found the drug's effects to be rewarding and pleasurable. That is, taking the drug improved your emotional state or mood, or made you feel more relaxed and less anxious, or more alert and energetic, or made you feel smarter or more attractive or more personable. In which case, you will probably decide that you like the drug's effects, and you will likely try using the drug again. The abuse liability of the drug for any individual, is directly related to the magnitude or intensity of the euphoric reaction of that individual following the self-administration of the drug.

Drug Tolerance:

Repetitions of drug-taking are an important part of the drug addiction process. Each time you take the drug, you are exposing your brain to the drug's effects. And, the drug's effects on your brain may change with repeated applications of the drug, so you may note systematic alterations and adjustments in your neurophysiological and behavioral reactions that accompany repetitions of experiences with taking the drug. For example, the first time you use the drug you may experience an intense euphoric reaction or "rush", but this reaction may be noticeably less intensely pleasurable the second time the drug is taken, and this diminished euphoric effect is even further diminished by each subsequent experience with the use of the drug. This is tolerance. The development of tolerance to the drug's pleasurable effects typically develops rapidly, much to the dismay of the drug user, and this tolerance effect contributes greatly to the increase over time of the escalation of the doses of the drug that are self-administered, as the user pursues the ever more elusive "rush" (Solomon & Corbit, 1978).

The development of tolerance to the drug's euphoric effects, due to repetitions of drug use, may result in the user adjusting upward the dose of the drug that is self-administered. This, in turn, increases greatly the user's chances of experiencing chronically elevated exposures to higher doses of the drug, which sets the stage for the development of drug dependence and abstinence-induced withdrawal, the classic signs of the later stages drug addiction. Thus, repetitions of voluntary drug-taking typically lead to the development of tolerance which may contribute to the escalation of drug-taking that sets the stage for addiction.

Cue Reactivity:

Each repetition of drug-taking provides the user with a pairing of the environmental stimuli that are present at that time with the drug's rewarding effects, leading to Pavlovian conditioning effects that may contribute to the development of drug addiction (Carter & Tiffany, 1999; Rohsenow, et al., 1994; Stewart, et al., 1984). That is, repetitions of drug-taking, in the presence of the same environmental stimuli, again and again, may lead to Pavlovian conditioning of emotional reactions and physiological reactions that come to be elicited by the mere presence of these drug-associated cues. In this way, the presence of your drinking pals, in the local tavern, with the bottle of your favorite beer, etc., will become increasingly likely to elicit conditioned euphoria or conditioned feelings of pleasure and well-being, as well as conditioned release of a brain chemical, dopamine. And, this conditioned euphoria will add to the euphoria-inducing effects of the alcohol itself. Thus, drinking beer from the bottle while in the tavern with your pals will be especially enjoyable and will likely become a favorite activity.

Repetitions of drug-taking in the presence of the same familiar stimuli strengthens the conditioning of euphoria and dopamine release in response to these drug-associated cues, which, in turn, serve to enhance the pleasure you derive from drug-taking in those situations. It is not at all surprising, therefore, that drug use is likely to become more and more highly repetitive, more and more practiced in the same way, in the same location, in the presence of the same people.

Taken to the extreme, drug-taking will evolve into a narrowly practiced ritual (Grund, 1993, Stahl, 1995). Due to repeated acts of ritualized drug-taking, drug associated cues will become more and more empowered to trigger not only emotional reactions but also motor activation responses of reflexive and target-directed responding. Cue-elicited motor activation will encourage the drug user to automatically move about, to explore and investigate the drug use environment, searching for the drug reward. But, these drug cue-elicited motor actions are reflexive and involuntary actions that are not under voluntary control, that may contribute to the poorly controlled drug-taking actions that plague the drug addict.

Incentive Salience:

Repetitions of drug-taking also produce another effect that may contribute to the development of drug addiction. Even as tolerance develops, even as the drug's rewarding effects are systematically diminished by repeated acts of drug-taking, the user becomes more and more reactive to the drug-associated cues that become more and more effective in evoking emotional feelings of "wanting" and "craving" and "needing" the drug. That is, the stimuli associated with drug-taking become brighter, more noticeable, more salient, more provocative, and more potent as motivational incentives. When in the presence of these stimuli, the addict will experience overwhelming desires to experience the drug's effects, to get high, even though, due to tolerance, the drug effects are less and less pleasurable (Robinson & Berridge, 1993, 2000).

Some individuals will claim that they were immediately addicted to the drug, from their very first experience with the drug. These individuals say they experienced overwhelming feelings of euphoria after taking the drug for the first time, and based on the sheer intensity of their euphoria, they were certain that they would again decide to re-administer the drug. Just to be clear, they are not saying that they are already hopelessly addicted. They are saying that they were certain that they would decide to take the drug again. But, feeling that you know with certainty that you will decide to repeat the act of voluntarily taking the drug is not the same as being addicted to the drug.

You are not addicted merely because you intensely enjoy the drug's effects. You are addicted if you cannot stop yourself. You are addicted if you automatically perform the action of taking the drug, even though you are explicitly instructing yourself, even begging yourself, not to do it. You are addicted if you specifically intend to refrain from drug-taking, but you take the drug anyway. Those individuals who enormously like the drug's effects may be more inclined to re-administer the drug, and this may eventually contribute greatly to their tendency to subsequently become addicted, but at the beginning, on their first use, they are not there yet. It takes repetitions of acts of voluntary drug-taking to get to the point where the act of drug-taking becomes unstoppable.

Chapter 5: The Stumble

According to addiction researchers, it is through repetition and ritual that drug-taking gradually shifts from what initially started out as a strictly voluntary action to something that more closely resembles an acquired triggered reflex (Tiffany, 1990; Tomie, 1995, 1996). The first indication that things are changing in this way is evident when you find yourself performing the act of taking the drug, even though, on reflection, you realize that you did not actually decide to do it. In other words, you did not form the specific intention to take the drug, and you have no conscious awareness of deciding to do it, but regardless, you watch yourself performing the action of reaching out and then consuming the drug. This is particularly likely to happen during an ongoing episode of drug-taking, when you are in the presence of drug-associated cues that trigger the performance of the actions of drug-taking, making it more difficult to apply the brakes. This is not the same as changing your mind about stopping or abstaining. This is performing an action without intending to do it. This is the first sign of trouble.

Action Without Intention:

This scenario typically plays out when you have that extra drink, one more than intended, and you do it automatically, without giving it a thought. For example, while headed to the local tavern with some friends, you state your specific intention to stop after having a couple of drinks. Though your plan was to stop after your second drink, while seated at the bar and without thinking about the limit you announced, you automatically nod to the bartender when he points at your empty glass. Still later that same night, the damage comes in at four drinks, though you have no conscious awareness of forming the decision to have the third or the fourth. Nevertheless, it is obvious to all that you in fact did have those drinks, both of which have been added to your tab.

In thinking about it, you distinctly recall deciding to have the first two drinks, both of which, therefore, were voluntary and intended acts of drug-taking. No problem. But what about the third and fourth drinks? Their origins were more out of thin air. They "just sort of happened". Note that the voice of the narration changes from first person to third person, indicating that somehow, you were less than fully in the moment. The third and fourth drinks "just happened". Perhaps, arguably, you were in fact a bit distracted, but regardless of engrossing conversations or mesmerizing passages of music or pretty faces or any other excuses, it was you who performed those acts of drug-taking. Admittedly, they did occur in the background of your conscious awareness, so you have no clear recollections of them, but nevertheless, they did "happen", and it was you who did them. The lesson here is that all acts of drug-taking are not the same. Some acts of drug-taking are more voluntary than others (Tomie, 1995). The first two drinks were strictly voluntary, but the next two, the third and fourth drinks were consumed, but more automatically, out of routine and habit, than anything else. Though "having another" is something that "just happened", the question remains, "Why didn't I stop after two drinks, like I intended?"

Involuntary Drug-Taking:

Your intuition is your "flying by the seat of your pants" best guess, street-wise, navigation guide … the repository of your collected wisdom accumulated from your first-hand experiences dealing with life. When called to answer for those two extra drinks, your intuition tells you, "You changed your mind. You decided to have another." This is because, in reviewing your inventory of your drug-taking history, all of your prior acts of drug-taking were voluntary and intended; therefore, the third and fourth drinks, by default, were also of this sort. Though you did have a couple more drinks than you originally intended, your intuition can only see both of those extra drinks as intended. For this to be the case, you must have changed your mind, reversing course about the two drink limit. You simply changed your mind about stopping at two.

In other words, when you ask your intuition to account for your action, your intuition forms a conclusion based on your prior experiences. Because all your previous acts of drug-taking, all of them, were voluntary and intended, your intuition, by default is hemmed in. This latest instance of drug-taking must be more of the same, because, after all, there is nothing else. It is all too easy to shoehorn that conclusion into the pre-existing narrative, that all drug-taking is necessarily a voluntary act that is performed because it is intended.

Based on your past experiences with drug-taking, your intuition is totally unaware of and is completely oblivious to the existence of automatic, reflexive, or involuntary drug-taking. And unless provided with information indicating otherwise, your intuition can only misguide you into erroneously concluding that the third and fourth drinks were voluntary and intended, when, in fact, they were not. In this way, the emerging evidence of your loss of self-control of your drug-taking, slips by unnoticed, allowing you to proceed as though you remain in control and nothing has changed. Is it not shameful that your trusted intuition would beguile you from coming to terms with a loss so deeply personal and unexpected? Unfair as it is, this allows automatic and reflexive and out-of-control drug-taking to proceed unchecked, to strengthen further, increasing the chances that this will end badly.

Testing Your Self-Control:

The problem is that involuntary drug-taking looks just exactly like the voluntary act of drug-taking. How can you determine if you are in control of your drug-taking? This is an empirical question that requires an observable standard or heuristic, to serve as a rule of thumb. Here it is. You are in control of your drug-taking if you decide to refrain and you stop at that point, immediately. No excuses. Regardless of the half empty glass sitting in front of you. Regardless of the need to celebrate or to be sociable, or to be a pal. You are in control of your drug-taking if you do in fact stop when you intended to stop. You are not negotiating with yourself. You are evaluating your control of your drug-taking. You are not in control of your drug-taking if you decide to refrain or set a limit, but later, when facing temptation, you "change your mind". "Changing your mind" is not allowed. If you "change your mind", then you have utterly failed the test. "Changing your mind" is the very essence of self-control failure. Having a drink after "changing your mind" is an involuntary drug-taking act. This is the stumble.

Chapter 6: Falling Into Addiction

At this point, you are beginning to experience automatic acts of drug-taking ... acts of drug-taking that were not intended but somehow happened anyway. You are headed for trouble. The unforeseen problem is that each act of automatic drug-taking provides the pairing arrangement that encourages another, further strengthening automatic and unintended acts of drug-taking. Meanwhile, the user still likes his drug and continues to perform voluntary acts of drug-taking, as before, but now, in addition, taking the drug without giving it a thought is also happening, side by side, and with greater and greater frequency.

These two very different types of acts of drug-taking, voluntary in contrast to reflexive, merge into a single unified stream, resulting in excessive levels of drug-taking, where more drug is consumed than was intended. The increasing frequency of binge episodes of excessive and poorly controlled drug-taking is the tell. As control of drug-taking slips further and further out of reach, the user remains steadfast and unconcerned. Due to the limitations of intuitive knowledge, the user is only aware of voluntary drug-taking, leading the user to erroneously conclude, by default, that all drug-taking is voluntary and intended … after all, that is all that there is. Taking drugs to excess is, therefore, regrettable but correctable … the remedy is simply a matter of making better decisions, going forward. The problem of bad decision-making will be resolved by not allowing the bad decisions to happen in the future.

Action Despite Intention:

Realistically, things have been headed in the wrong direction for some time now, and it should come as no surprise that things are about to get worse. The next step in the drug addiction process is when you instruct yourself not to take the drug, but you do it anyway. This is a level of self-control failure that is far more troubling than just mindlessly taking the drug without intending to do it, because this is drug-taking that is in direct defiance of your specific intention to abstain. This is deeply disturbing because it makes no sense that you would do it while instructing yourself not to.

How does this happen? How do you get to this point, where you simply cannot stop yourself? This happens because unintended acts of drug-taking, dozens of them, were misconstrued as voluntary acts of drug-taking, misleading you into believing that you remained firmly in control when you were not. This false belief in the illusion of self-control encouraged you to move along unconcerned, while changing nothing and continuing as before, leaving you to repeat exactly what gave rise to automatic and unintended drug-taking in the first place. This will encourage additional involuntary acts of drug-taking to take place with even greater frequency, as control of drug-taking spins further and further out of reach. Each act of automatic drug-taking increases the likelihood of another, strengthening automatic drug-taking to the point where self-control is simply overwhelmed.

Drug addicts often complain bitterly that they do not understand why they cannot quit. They say they are trying desperately to quit, and more than anything else in the world, they want their life back, but, inexplicably, as much as they want to quit, they continue to take the drug. They are scared and confused and frustrated because this reality does not fit their expectations. According to their understanding of how things work, all along they were taking the drug because they wanted to do it, and their expectation was that one of these days, sometime in the future, they would decide to quit. And when they decided to quit, that would be the end of it. After quitting, they would go on with their lives, with drugs in the rearview mirror. They never imagined that they could decide to quit and then not be able to. But, repeated failed attempts to stop using, left them flabbergasted, astonished, horrified, and afraid. How can this be happening to me? I am trying to quit. Why can't I stop?

Self-Control Failure:

The compulsion to take drugs against your will is a complicated topic, made more confusing by the later appearance of symptoms of drug dependence and abstinence-induced withdrawal, particularly for abusers of opiates, alcohol, and benzodiazepines. Drug addicts who experience drug dependence and withdrawal symptoms complain of getting "drug sick" if they abstain from drug-taking, and this sickness is quickly alleviated by taking the drug. Drug sickness constitutes an extremely effective deterrent against quitting drug use.

Dependence and withdrawal are well-known as classic signs of drug addiction, but they are observed in the later stages of the drug addiction process. Just to be clear, the loss of self-control of drug-taking due to the development of automatic and reflexive performance of acts of drug-taking, is not the same as getting drug sick. Well before the earliest development of dependence and withdrawal symptoms, and even though they are not yet acquainted with what it is to become "drug sick", many drug abusers complain that they tried to escape the drug life but were astounded to discover that they were unable to quit. They tried to quit, but when faced with the temptation of drugs, they found that they could not abstain. They failed at quitting, time and again. They could not bring themselves to quit because they felt compelled to use the drug, and this had nothing to do with becoming drug sick. This happened well before they had developed any of the symptoms of drug dependence or abstinence-induced withdrawal, so their capitulation to use the drug was not compelled by drug-sickness. It was something else. When in the drug-taking space, when surrounded by the presence of drug-associated cues, they experienced the overwhelming compulsion to take the drug.

Addicts vividly describe their feelings of being overwhelmed when in the presence of cues that indicate that drug-taking is close at hand. This is due to physiological and neurobiological reactions that anticipate the delivery of the drug to the brain that alter their sense of conscious and cognitive awareness. At the same time, brain control of complex, directed motor sequences shift into gear. Ancient survival reflexes buried deep in the midbrain are activated. The addict is swept along by instructions to approach the drug, contact the drug, and consume the drug. The addict is a passive observer of their own actions. The addict can only watch as they take the drug despite the best of intentions and the firmest of self-instructed admonitions not to do it. Performing the action of drug-taking despite the intention not to do it is horrifying and deeply disturbing. It is other-worldly, incomprehensible, and often accompanied by screaming and crying, hand wringing and head-holding. It reveals the naked truth … that drug-taking is completely out of control. At this point, things have gone way too far. You are helpless to stop yourself from taking the drug and your intentions to quit are meaningless. Your drug-taking is completely out of control. You are a drug addict.

Chapter 7: The Brain and Reward

Abused drugs act on the brain, and repeated use of the drug alters the brain's response to the drug. According to Nora Volkow, Chief of the National Institute on Drug Abuse (NIDA), addiction is a brain disease (Volkow, et al., 2016). That is, repeated administrations of an abused drug produce long-lasting changes in the brain that underlie the self-control failure of the drug addict (Leshner, 1997). In this section, we will describe the very basic brain substrates of reward and addiction. We will focus on the brain's reward processing circuit, the ascending mesolimbic dopamine pathway with cell bodies located in the ventral tegmentum and its primary axonal projection to an area of the brain called the nucleus accumbens (NAC).

A rewarding experience is accompanied by an emotional state, often described as a feeling of pleasure, satisfaction, well-being, or euphoria. Scientists have determined that these feelings, these subjective emotional states, are associated with elevated neuronal activity or elevated firing rates of neurons in an area of the brain called the nucleus accumbens (NAC). For this reason, the NAC is often called the reward center or pleasure center of the brain. The activity level in the NAC is associated with the amount or levels of a brain chemical, or neurotransmitter, called dopamine (DA). An elevated level of DA activity in the NAC is associated with the positive emotional state typically described as "pleasure" (Wise, 2004). For example, eating food when hungry induces the release of DA in the NAC, which is accompanied by subjective reports of feelings of pleasure, satisfaction, and enjoyment.

Natural Rewards:

Food, water, and sex are natural rewards. Each of these natural rewards produces an increase in DA activity levels in NAC that are associated with subjective experiences of feelings of pleasure and euphoria (Kelley & Berridge, 2002). The elevated DA activity in NAC also produces other effects, beyond feeling good. For example, elevated DA activity in NAC also activates a learning or association process. The environmental stimuli that are also present at the time that DA activation occurs in the NAC are identified as possible causes of the positive emotional state produced by the natural reward. That is, in addition to producing feelings of pleasure, DA activation in the NAC also produces connections or associations to stimuli in the environment (people, places, things, sounds, etc.) that were present at the time of the euphoric episode (Day & Carelli, 2007).

In addition, the elevated DA activity in the NAC also produces an effect on motor responding that looks like an investigatory reflex. Scientists call this response "psychomotor activation". In response to reward, the subject becomes excited, aroused, and active, moving about, on the lookout, searching for more reward. Thus, natural rewards induce elevated DA neurotransmission in the NAC, which, in turn produces three different types of effects: feelings of pleasure, the association of the experience of pleasure with stimuli present at that time, and skeletal-motor responses of the psychomotor activation syndrome. It is the interplay among these three functions of the integrated reward system, each of which arises from the activation of the NAC, that form the major features of the rewarding experience.

The Integrated Reward System:

The functional biological significance of each of the features of the integrated reward system warrants further discussion:

What is the functional biological significance of pleasure? Pleasure is the neurobiological mechanism of reward identification, which is the brain's way of marking the things in the environment that you must pursue. Food, water, and sex are natural rewards, pursuit of which are essential to survival. The pleasure reaction elicited by these natural rewards, through their activation of DA in the NAC, serves to increase the likelihood that these natural rewards will be pursued.

What is the functional biological significance of learning? Learning is the process of associating the feelings of pleasure with stimuli in the environment that are predictive of the feelings of pleasure. Association is the brain's way of figuring out which of those external stimuli in the environment is the most likely cause of the pleasure. Association is the brain's target identification process. The brain is looking to assign blame or credit. Stimuli that are more highly predictive of pleasure are more likely to be blamed or credited as the root cause of the pleasure, and these environmental stimuli become identified as high-valued targets.

What is the functional biological significance of psychomotor activation? Psychomotor activation is the brain's reward guidance system. Psychomotor activation is the target-directed sequence of motor activation responses elicited by reward, which provides the brain with information related to the appraisal of possible targets, based on their salience or their relative attractiveness, as possible targets. Target identification leads to target selection, followed by approach the target, contact the target, and then consume the target. Said another way, "I just got reward. I want more. Where is it?" Psychomotor activation is the automatic performance of target-directed responses designed to increase the chances of finding the source of the reward and then consuming it.

The Prehistoric Beast:

How do the integrated functions of the reward system work together to increase the chances that an individual will survive? Consider the story of the starving prehistoric beast. The ancient beast is on the verge of starvation. Food is scarce and the beast could use some help figuring out where it is. The famished beast picks up a small oblong beige object, looks at it closely, then chews and swallows it. Fortunately, it happens to be a grain of wheat, a food reward that is filled with nutrients, calories, and dietary amino acids. These food reward nutrients activate the NAC. The brain's integrated reward system kicks into play, automatically giving rise to feelings of pleasure, accompanied by a pattern of motor activity, psychomotor activation, as the beast searches for more food rewards. The beast just ate a nutritious piece of food. Psychomotor activation is the pattern of physical motor activity that automatically flows forth, to organize the process of searching for more food.

Psychomotor activation begins with an investigation of the environment. The beast may stand erect, rearing and sniffing, looking around, visually scanning, evaluating the environment for features of interest – namely food. But the food is laying on the ground, scattered about amongst stones, dirt, twigs, and other non-food items. But, because the grain of wheat was the last item that the beast looked at, in the course of eating, and just before NAC activation, this oblong beige food object is the thing that is most likely associated by the NAC with strong feelings of pleasure. The association of the grain of wheat with the emotional state of pleasure will improve the chances that the grain of wheat will be selected as the target of the psychomotor activation syndrome. The beast approaches the second grain of wheat, picks up the grain of wheat, and consumes the grain of wheat, then the beast experiences a jolt of DA activation in the NAC, accompanied by feelings of pleasure.

The story continues. The hungry beast locates on the ground nearby another small beige oblong object … another grain of wheat. Psychomotor activation automatically leads the beast to approach the grain of wheat, pick it up and eat it. After eating the third grain of wheat, the beast experiences another jolt of DA activation in the NAC. This is accompanied by another pleasure reaction, which is experienced right after seeing the grain of wheat, resulting in even more of a connection or association between the wheat grain and feelings of pleasure. In this way, each grain of wheat becomes more tightly associated with pleasure, encouraging the beast to approach, contact, and eat the wheat grain. Thanks to the integrated reward system, the beast has automatically "figured out" what to eat.

Note that activating the integrated reward system reduces the complex process of identifying food, then finding and eating food, into a largely automatic and reflexive, targeted action sequence that serves to improve the chances of surviving in a patchy world of scarce food resources. The beast survives, increasing the chances of reproductive success and transmitting this trait, the integrated reward system, to successive generations of progeny. Fast forward to the present. Evolution has done its job, equipping the brains of modern beasts with the integrated reward system, deployed by NAC activation to aid in survival. When we experience reward, we experience the emotion of pleasure, the association of the pleasure with stimuli in the environment that are present at that time, and the psychomotor activation pattern of target-directed approach, contact, and consume.

Addictive Drugs:

What does all of this have to do with drug addiction? According to Nora Volkow, abused drugs hijack the brain's reward system (Volkow, et al., 2011). Abused drugs are not natural rewards, but all drugs of abuse, including alcohol, cocaine, amphetamine, barbiturates, nicotine, marijuana, opiates, etc., share one common intersection in their neurobiological mechanisms of action. All abused drugs activate the same DA NAC reward pathway that are activated by natural rewards such as food, water, and sex. And, abused drugs are often far better than natural reward at doing this. The magnitude of the activation of DA in the NAC by abused drugs may be exponentially greater than the effect produced by even the most potent of natural rewards. In this way, drugs of abuse hijack the reward system, diverting the system away from sub-serving their intended survival function, and toward the sub-serving of addictive behaviors.

What does the integrated reward system have to do with drug addiction? Consider the story of Johnny having a drink. Johnny is a moderate, social drinker. He enjoys having a few beers with his friends to relax after work. Lately, however, he has noticed that his beer intake has been gradually increasing, so that instead of having two beers at the poker game, he drinks four beers, or more. Drinking beer is pleasurable and mood-improving because the alcohol in the beer produces elevated DA activity in the NAC. In addition, activation of the NAC leads Johnny to associate other stimuli present at that time with these positive feelings, so that Johnny feels good at the bar, or at the poker game, hanging out with his drinking pals. The NAC associates the people, places, and things that are present while drinking beer, with the positive feelings of beer-induced euphoria.

The stimulus that is likely to be most closely associated with DA activation of the NAC is Johnny's beer bottle. This is because Johnny sees the beer bottle in those moments in time just before the alcohol in the beer activates the NAC in Johnny's brain. The strong association between the beer bottle and the activation of DA in the NAC will cause the beer bottle to become a high-value target of the psychomotor activation syndrome. This means that Johnny's attention will be guided toward the beer bottle because the beer bottle, due to its association with alcohol reward, is a feature of the environment that Johnny finds salient, attention-grabbing, and attractive. When Johnny sees the beer bottle he immediately feels better, and the magnetic force of attraction tugs at him and pulls him to the location of the beer bottle, where he will reflexively reach out, take the beer bottle in his hands, then hold and drink from the beer bottle.

But the beer consumed in this way, due to the psychomotor activation syndrome, is not the same as the beer that is consumed as a voluntary, intended, decision-based response. The psychomotor activation syndrome is an automatic and involuntary response coming out of a primitive survival reflex activated by the NAC in the deep regions of the prehistoric midbrain. Psychomotor activation is not an intended action. Johnny did not decide to drink some more beer. Johnny is drinking beer on automatic pilot. In this way, the integrated reward system leads Johnny, mindlessly and thoughtlessly, to have another beer. Johnny is beginning to stumble, losing control, having more beers than intended. His excessive beer drinking is happening automatically, due to the integrated functions of the reward system.

In the chapters to follow, you will be introduced to sign-tracking, which is a behavioral phenomenon identified by scientists that provides a model of the loss of self-control. Sign-tracking is induced by Pavlovian pairings of an object with a reward. Sign-tracking is an acquired Pavlovian reflexive response that consists of a targeted, motor action sequence that is directed at the object that predicts the reward. As detailed in the following chapters, sign-tracking provides a model of several prominent symptoms of drug addiction (Tomie, 1995, 1996; Tomie et al., 2008).

Chapter 8: Sign-Tracking

In our view, the root cause of drug addiction is the loss of self-control of drug-taking. The essence of the problem of drug addicts is that they are unable to control their drug-taking. They take the drug even when they are telling themselves not to do it. To gain a better understanding of drug addiction, we must account for this key aspect of the disorder. One particularly promising approach, based on Pavlovian sign-tracking, has been developed by addiction research scientists working in the experimental behavioral analytics laboratory (Tomie, 1995, 1996, 2018b) and in the wet-lab environment of the addiction neurobiologist (Flagel, et al., 2007; Robinson, et al., 2018).

It Makes No Sense:

What is sign-tracking? Right from the beginning, it should be mentioned that many observers have reported that sign-tracking is a bit confusing and difficult to grasp, at least initially. And this is not because sign-tracking is so complicated, but, rather because sign-tracking is counterintuitive. Interested readers are encouraged to preview a brief video of sign-tracking behavior in a laboratory rat, https://www.youtube.com/watch?v=x38b0R6TZxM.

Many students working on research projects in my lab, upon seeing sign-tracking for the first time, are befuddled, perplexed, and confused. They are watching a simple sign-tracking experiment in which the subject, a laboratory rat, experiences the brief insertion of a small lever into the test chamber. The insertion of the lever signals that food reward will soon be delivered. After 5 sec, the lever is retracted from the chamber and a small food pellet is delivered into the food tray. Important to the understanding of sign-tracking, the food pellet is delivered on each trial regardless of what the rat does. The hungry rat reacts to the delivery of the food by running over to the location of the food tray, where the hungry rat picks up the food pellet and eats it. This is the sign-tracking procedure, the pairing of an object (lever) with a reward (food), such that the object signals that reward is on the way. This procedure gives rise to the sign-tracking response. Each pairing of lever and food is separated from the next sign-tracking trial, the next lever-food pairing, by about a minute. It takes about 20 trials, each consisting of a lever-food pairing, for the rat to develop the sign-tracking response.

The sign-tracking response is quite simple. The rat behaves toward the lever as though it were the food. The rat's behavior strongly suggests that the rat has learned to associate the insertion of the lever with the delivery of the food. The rat approaches the lever, then grasps the lever with the forepaws, and then the rat licks and gnaws the lever. Just to be clear, the lever is made of chrome stainless steel and has no nutritional value. Nevertheless, the insertion of the lever triggers the rat to quickly respond by performing a complex sequence of motor actions that are directed at the lever. These motor actions resemble the responses that are directed by the rat at the food. Put another way, it appears that the rat is attempting to eat the lever. But, to be clear, these actions serve no purpose and are a complete waste of time and energy. Moreover, the rat appears to be incapable of figuring it out, doing it more and more on trial after trial.

Students in my research lab, watching the rat acquire and maintain sign-tracking responses, are initially amused, but their smiles eventually give way to furrowed brows and looks of consternation. They are thoroughly befuddled and perplexed. While pointing at the rat, they ask each other and then finally they ask me, "Why is the rat doing this?" When I answer that the rat is sign-tracking due to lever-food pairings, they nod in agreement, indicating that they know about sign-tracking. But then they respond with, "Okay, I get that, but what's the point of their doing that?" while waving their hand in the direction of the rat at the lever. The students are requesting a more satisfying explanation, for the rat eating the lever. They are asking for an account that makes more sense. They are asking for an explanation that connects the sign-tracking response to a purpose or a goal or a reason for doing it. The lever-food pairing explanation is correct, as far as it goes, but from the student's point of view, sign-tracking makes no sense.

One of my more inquisitive students, after spending considerably more time intently observing the behavior of the rat, suddenly declared, "I got it! The rat contacts the lever, and then, after contacting the lever, the rat gets the food. The rat wants the food, and getting the food happens soon after contacting the lever. So, the rat thinks that contacting the lever causes the food to be delivered." Note that the student has framed the rat's behavior so that the behavior of contacting the lever is connected to a goal or purpose ... contacting the lever serves the purpose of obtaining food. Note also, that to accept this explanation, the student must selectively disregard all of the evidence that is inconsistent with this hypothesis ... that is, all the times that the student saw the rat receive the food even though the rat did not contact the lever. And this happened many times, particularly at the beginning of the experiment.

Clearly, the student is more prepared to accept some observations as compared to others. The student is willing to accept and process and retain those observations that are consistent with the guidance provided by his pre-existing intuition, which tells him that the behavior of the rat is goal directed. The lesson here is that the student is observing sign-tracking in the laboratory and processing these observations of sign-tracking to fit his pre-conceived framework, that behavior is performed for a reason, to fulfill a purpose. A similar error happens in the tavern, where the drug user is challenged to understand their automatic and unintended acts of drug-taking. In both cases, the student and the drug user are not comfortable until they are able to account for their observations as voluntary and intended goal directed behaviors. This is the stumble. This is where we go off-track. This is where we adopt the false premise that sign-tracking is voluntary. This is where we fall for the illusion that we are in control of our drug-taking.

Sign-tracking is difficult to grasp because sign-tracking is counterintuitive. When we see sign-tracking, our intuition tells us that we are seeing a voluntary motor action, a voluntary goal-directed response, that is performed for a reason, to fulfill a purpose, in order to get something out of it. But the scientific evidence says, in the case of sign-tracking, our intuition is incorrect. The scientific evidence says that the sign-tracking response is not a voluntary response. Even though sign-tracking admittedly resembles a voluntary intended action, the scientific evidence firmly supports an alternative conclusion … that the sign-tracking response is an acquired Pavlovian reflex. The consistent conclusion derived from dozens of carefully controlled scientific experiments is that the sign-tracking response is a Pavlovian conditioned reflex, that is acquired due to experience with repeated object-reward pairings (Tomie, et al., 1989). Note that the drug user experienced an object-reward pairing with each trial of voluntary drug self-administration, and then after dozens of drug-taking trials, the drug user finds that acts of unintended and automatic drug-taking are "just happening". The discovery of sign-tracking casts the unintended and poorly-controlled drug-taking behavior of the drug addict in an entirely different light.

Reflexive Responding:

Sign-tracking is not a voluntary goal-directed response. Sign-tracking is an acquired reflexive response. Reflexive responding differs greatly from voluntary responding. By way of example, suppose for a moment that you are working in the kitchen, near the cooktop. Without looking, you reach for a plate, but your hand gets too close to the open flame.

Before you are aware of what has happened, in scarcely more than an instant, your hand has been pulled back, out of harm's way, and well before you suffered even a mild burn. Your hand was saved from injury by the activation of a pain or nociceptive reflex. Pain receptors in your hand sensed the heat, then immediately triggered the muscles in your hand and arm to contract, removing your hand from the flame.

This is not a voluntary response. This is a reflexive response. It occurred automatically. You did not decide to remove your hand from the flame. Your hand was out of the flame before you even realized it was in there. The reflex took place without your knowledge, without your consent, and without your awareness. It was mindless, thoughtless, and involuntary. You could not stop it. You could not intercede with grim determination to force your hand to remain in the flame. You could not thwart the reflex, or over-ride the reflex, or impose your will on the reflex. You were a passive observer of the reflex, like a passenger on the train, rolling down the tracks. The reflexive response is an automatic and involuntary action that occurs quickly and without your awareness, whether you like it or not.

We are born into the world with innate hard-wired reflexes, such as the nociceptive pain reflex described above. Our repertoire of reflexive responses is not fixed and forever limited to those that are hard-wired. We may develop additional reflexive responses that are learned or conditioned by our experiences with the organization of the world that we live in. That is, a new reflexive response may be acquired or learned via a conditioning process. Sign-tracking is an acquired reflex that develops due to a Pavlovian conditioning process. Pavlov's dogs received tone-food pairings, from which they came to associate the tone with the food. Pavlov's dogs learned to react to the presentation of the tone signal by reflexively salivating, behaving to the tone as though the tone was food. In the case of sign-tracking, the insertion of the lever signals the delivery of the food, and the rat learns to react to the presentation of the lever by reflexively eating the lever, as though the lever was the food.

The Sign-Tracking Reflex:

Before proceeding further, a few more general comments about sign-tracking are appropriate. It should be noted that sign-tracking is a classic example of a basic science find. The discovery of sign-tracking by Brown and Jenkins (1968) came about due to their conducting a basic science study, an experimental inquiry in the animal learning laboratory, of the effects of previously well-studied experimental factors, but they combined these factors in a unique way. The results of their experiments were totally surprising and completely unexpected. The discovery of sign-tracking made a huge splash in the conditioning and learning field in large part because sign-tracking contradicted many of the most time-honored and fundamental tenets of traditional learning theory (Locurto, et al., 1981; Tomie, 2018a). Sign-tracking is important because it changed our view of the behavioral universe. Sign-tracking was not anticipated or expected or intended, and not always welcomed, for that matter. Particularly early on, there were those who objected strenuously to sign-tracking. But, the thing about a science find is, like it or not, it is still true. Sign-tracking was outside the expected, and the unexpected, very much like the unintended, is more readily rejected because it is more difficult to absorb. Nevertheless, the reward of science is the discovery of the unexpected.

Reports of sign-tracking are certainly not an oddity. There are now, in the published scientific literature, hundreds of experimental studies documenting sign-tracking, though sign-tracking is often referred to as "autoshaping" (Brown & Jenkins, 1968; Locurto, et al., 1981) or "Pavlovian conditioned approach" (Domjan, et al., 1986) or "conditioned approach" (Cunningham & Patel, 2007). The vast majority of the published experimental literature on sign-tracking employed Pavlovian delay conditioning procedures to train animal subjects, mainly pigeons or rats, though many other species are also reported to exhibit sign-tracking responses (for reviews, see Locurto, et al. 1981; Tomie, et al., 1989; Joyner, et al., 2018). With varying degrees of success, sign-tracking performance has been documented in birds (pigeons, ring doves, finches, domestic chickens, chicks, and quail), and mammals (rats, mice, hamsters, guinea pigs, gerbils, horses, dogs, and cats), and amphibians (frogs), and reptiles (monitor lizards and turtles), and fish (tilapia fish, goldfish, blue gourami, cuttlefish, sharks, halibut, and cod), and non-human primates (cynomolgus monkeys, rhesus monkeys, and squirrel monkeys), and human beings (human children and human adults).

Sign-tracking has also been induced by a wide range of rewarding stimuli, including response-independent delivery of access to a solid food (grain pellets, mixed grains, mash), access to a sipper tube containing a liquid solution (water, saccharin, sucrose), access to a sipper tube containing a solution of an abused drug (alcohol, cocaine, chlordiazepoxide, opiates), access to warmth provided by a radiant heat source, access to brief social interaction opportunity with a conspecific, or with a sexual partner, delivery of rewarding electrical brain stimulation, and injection or infusion of an abused drug, including cocaine, opiates, amphetamines, or benzodiazepines.

Sign-Tracking and Drug Reward:

Of particular relevance to the application of sign-tracking to drug addiction, there are numerous published experiments indicating that presenting an object, typically a lever, that predicts the rewarding effects of an abused drug, will reliably induce sign-tracking responses that are directed at the lever (for review, see Tomie, 2018b). For example, presenting a lever followed by an injection of cocaine induced rats to approach the lever and sniff the lever, even though the cocaine was delivered regardless of what the subject did (Uslaner, et al., 2006). Other investigators have reported that presenting the lever as a signal for an infusion of cocaine induced rats to approach the lever and press the lever, even though neither response was necessary to receive the administration of cocaine (Carroll, et al., 2002; Flagel, et al., 2010). Using similar procedures, Carroll and Lac (1997) reported that pairing the insertion of a lever with an injection of amphetamine induced rats to press the lever, while other investigators have reported that pairing the insertion of a lever with an injection of heroin induced rats to press the lever (Lynch & Carroll, 1999; Roth, et al., 2002). Similar effects are observed with alcohol. Pairing the insertion of a lever with the presentation of a sipper tube filled with alcohol induced rats to press the lever, even though the alcohol sipper was delivered regardless of what the subject did (Tomie, 2001; Tomie, et al., 2002).

Sign-tracking responses are induced by pairing a light cue with access to an abused drug. For example, illumination of a light cue above a sipper tube filled with a cocaine solution provided rats with pairings of the light cue with cocaine's rewarding effects, and induced rats to approach the location of the light cue (Di Ciano & Everitt, 2003; Falk & Lau, 1993, 1995). Locating the light cue at a distance from the cocaine sipper supported a sign-tracking interpretation, as the rats continued to approach the light cue rather than the location of the cocaine sipper (Falk & Lau, 1993, 1995). Pairing the brief illumination of a cue light with alcohol drinking induced approach to the location of the cue light (Falk, 1994; Falk & Lau, 1995; Krank, 2003; Krank, et al., 2008) and also resulted in elevated performance of a voluntary response that was required to obtain access to alcohol drinking (Krank, 2003; Krank, et al., 2008). Pairing the intermittent insertion and retraction of a sipper tube filled with alcohol induced elevated alcohol drinking from the sipper tube relative to controls receiving continuous access to the sipper tube filled with alcohol, indicating that the positive contingency between the sipper tube signal and the alcohol solution induced sign-tracking of alcohol drinking (Tomie, et al., 2006; for review see Tomie & Sharma, 2013). Thus, addiction scientists have extensively documented that an object that signals drug reward will induce object-directed sign-tracking responses.

Pavlovian Approach and Drug Addiction:

An important feature of sign-training is that the subject is freely moving, an arrangement that is atypical of Pavlovian conditioning procedures. The freely-moving subject receives repetitions of an object that precedes the delivery of a reward, and the subject is free to adjust their location in response to these object-reward pairings in any way, including moving anywhere within the boundaries of the experimental chamber. The freely moving subject comes to develop a complex sequence, of signal-directed skeletal-motor orientations and actions. It is the targeting aspect of the response of the freely moving subject that allows sign-tracking behavior to uniquely model this potentially crucial feature of the drug addiction process. This includes the overwhelming, irresistible, attractiveness of drug-related cues that accompanies the habitual and automatic drug-taking of the drug abuser (Corbit & Janak, 2016; Robinson, et al., 2018; Robinson & Berridge, 1993). Sign-tracking procedures allow a form of expression of reflexive motor actions that model crucial features of the behavior of the freely moving drug addict that contribute to their vulnerability to the loss of self-control of drug-taking.

Sign-tracking responses serve to move the user into the vicinity of drug-use paraphernalia and drug-associated cues. These are the locations where the drug is present and likely to be used. When the user has been transported to the proximal presence of these drug-associated cues, the user is especially likely to experience cue reactivity effects (Carter & Tiffany, 1999; Stewart, et al., 1984). With respect to alcohol cues, for example, individuals differ in their reactions to the sight of their favorite alcoholic beverage. Those most tempted by the drug-associated cues reported stronger urges to drink alcohol and greater difficulty controlling urges, and these subjects also exhibited increased alcohol consumption (Palfai, 2001).

Cue reactivity effects include conditioned euphoric reactions, conditioned physiological reactions, and conditioned cravings and urges to experience alcohol's effects. These conditioned responses serve to increase the chances that the drug will be self-administered. This suggests that drug addiction is as much about the cues surrounding drug use as it is about the drug itself. This is not to deny the crucial role played by the drug itself, but, perhaps, the drug serves initially as the hook, but the cues are the barb of the hook that will not let go (Delmar, 2015). This much is clear. We are coming to understand that the attractiveness of drug cues, and in particular, the tools of drug-taking, play a major role in becoming hooked and in staying hooked (Di Ciano, & Everitt, 2004; Flagel, et al., 2009; Robinson & Berridge, 1993, 2000; Tomie, et al., 2016; Tomie & Sharma, 2013).

Common to many models of addictive behaviors is the premise that repeated drug self-administrations strengthen a Pavlovian, appetitive, cue approach-oriented system, resulting in automatic, reflexive responses that increase the performance of the action tendencies involved in approaching and consuming the drug (Dawe, et al., 2004; Jentsch & Taylor, 1999; Robinson & Berridge, 2003; Sherman, et al., 1989; Stewart, et al., 1984; Tiffany, 1990; Wiers, et al., 2007). According to these accounts, the Pavlovian responses elicited by the drug cues may include physiological reactions or subjective, emotional, and motivational states that serve to energize, direct, and propel the subject to perform the physical actions required to approach and consume the drug. It remains unclear, however, precisely how these Pavlovian physiological and emotional reactions elicited by drug-associated stimuli are transcribed into the target-directed, physical, skeletal-motor action sequences involved in moving the subject to the location of the reward cue and then consuming the drug.

Sign-tracking offers an intriguing fix to the problem of filling in the gap between emotional and physiological responses on the one hand and target-directed and consummatory actions on the other. In a sense, sign-tracking "cuts to the chase". Sign-tracking provides a Pavlovian, appetitive, drug-associated cue approach response, resulting in the performance of automatic, reflexive responses, that increase the directed action motor sequences involved in approaching and consuming the drug (Tomie, 1995, 1996; Tomie & Sharma, 2013). In this way, sign-tracking adds an essential and complementary piece to many existing Pavlovian cue reactivity models of addictive behaviors by delivering the subject to the drug-taking environment where the motor actions of consuming the drug are performed.

Chapter 9: The Loss of Self-Control

The essence of the problem of the drug addict is their inability to control their drug-taking. Sign-tracking provides a way of understanding how the loss of self-control of drug-taking may happen. In this chapter we will explore the evidence that experience with object-reward pairings compel the subject to perform sign-tracking responses that are difficult, if not impossible, for the subject to suppress or control.

Important to the understanding of sign-tracking, to obtain the food reward, the subject's performance of the sign-tracking response is completely unnecessary. This is because the subject receives the food reward on each trial, regardless of whether the subject performs or does not perform the sign-tracking response. Therefore, the sign-tracking response serves no purpose and is a complete waste of time and energy. For this reason, the performance of the sign-tracking response is a bit bizarre and may be construed as somewhat maladaptive. Performing the sign-tracking response makes little sense because approaching the lever only moves the subject away from the location of the tray where the food will soon be delivered. Thus, the sign-tracking response serves only to delay the opportunity to eat the food reward.

It seems reasonable to expect that if the subject were able to control the performance of the sign-tracking response, then the subject would simply stop doing it. But, subject after subject, in experiment after experiment, perform the sign-tracking response during trial after trial, even though the performance serves no purpose. These observations are the first of many that are consistent with the conclusion that the sign-tracking response is an acquired reflex, and, therefore, is not under the strict voluntary control of the subject.

Omission Training Studies:

To further investigate the possibility that the subject is unable to control the sign-tracking response, behavioral scientists performed additional experiments designed to discourage sign-tracking responses from developing in the first place. They altered the sign-tracking procedure so that, from the very beginning of the experiment, touching the lever was strictly prohibited. That is, the subject received the food reward on each trial, but the penalty for touching the lever was the cancellation or omission of the delivery of the food reward on that trial. Note that the only prohibited response is the sign-tracking response, and subjects have good reason not to do it, especially considering that all other responses are allowed. Nevertheless, sign-tracking studies employing these omission training procedures revealed that the sign-tracking response was quickly and reliably acquired and then maintained even in the face of an explicit omission training contingency designed specifically to prevent it from developing in the first place (Stiers & Silberberg, 1974; Williams & Williams, 1969; for review, see Locurto, 1981).

But this makes no sense. The subjects are hungry and want to eat. If able to do so, they would surely suppress their sign-tracking. Apparently, they cannot stop themselves. They perform the action even though their intention presumably is to not do it. We are left to conclude that the sign-tracking response is difficult, if not impossible, for the subject to control or suppress. Obviously, performing the only response that is prohibited, the only response that cancels the reward, which would otherwise be delivered, is maladaptive and counterproductive, and we have good reason to expect that, under these conditions, subjects would simply not perform the response. It is truly remarkable that rather than refrain subjects persist.

Sign-tracking performance is so persistent during omission training procedures that most subjects lose the larger share of the available rewards (Williams & Williams, 1969). Frankly, refraining from touching the lever that signals the delivery of the food reward does not seem like such a tall order. After all, subjects are pretty much allowed to do whatever they like, except, of course, touch the lever. Nevertheless, subjects cannot prevent themselves from performing the sign-tracking response despite receiving extensive training with losing the reward for doing so (for review, see Tomie, 1996). Sign-tracking is important because it provides us with a way of seeing how behavior can come to defy free-will … how the intention to abstain, to not perform the response, can be rendered meaningless. Sign-tracking provides us with a potentially crucial insight into the predicament of the drug addict, who continues to take the drug, even while pledging to quit.

The Compulsion to Respond:

Omission training studies provided the first of several lines of evidence showing that the sign-tracking response is largely refractory to a wide range of negative consequences that have been deployed in attempts to eliminate it. For example, sign-tracking responses develop and are maintained despite contingent shock punishment. In this study, the brief presentation of a visual cue light that signaled an intravenous infusion of cocaine induced sign-tracking of cue-directed approach responses (Uslaner, et al., 2006). The cocaine cue light was so irresistibly attractive that rats crossed an electrified grid floor to approach the location of a light cue that had previously been established as a signal for the operation of an infusion pump that delivered the intravenous cocaine injections. This effect was observed even though, during cocaine self-administration training, the sign-tracking response had no effect on the delivery of cocaine, and during the shock punishment test, the light cue was presented without infusions of cocaine.

Thus, the illumination of the cue light that had previously signaled cocaine infusion "goaded" the rats into crossing the shock grid even though there was no reason for the subject to run across the electrified grid floor, other than to approach the cocaine cue light. The rat was apparently overwhelmed by the sheer force of the magnetic attraction of the cocaine cue, which compelled the rat to suffer the pain of crossing the electrified grid floor, just to be closer to the light associated with the drug. Obviously, the aversive consequence of suffering self-inflicted painful electric shock was not sufficient to dissuade the rat from approaching the cocaine cue.

Long box studies (Hearst & Jenkins, 1974) provide further evidence of the compulsive nature of sign-tracking responses. In these studies, the brief illumination of a 1-in diameter translucent pecking key with a green light signal was paired with brief 5 sec access to a tray of mixed grain. The pigeons began to approach and peck the key light signal, performing the sign-tracking response, even though the key light was located at a distance from the food tray, so that pecking the key removed the pigeons from the vicinity of the food reward, thereby reducing the amount of time available to eat. Across trials, the distance separating the key light from the food tray was systematically increased, but subjects persisted in performing the sign-tracking response, even though key pecking was completely unnecessary. Finally, the key light was moved to a location so far away from the food tray that when the pigeons pecked the key light, they could not run to the food tray quickly enough to obtain any food.

On a trial of this sort, the key light was not followed by food, and this served to reduce the association between the key light and the food, as revealed by the extinction of the sign-tracking response. At this point, illuminating the key with the green light cue no longer induced the pigeon to run to peck the illuminated key light; however, by not pecking the key on that trial, the pigeon was able to eat the food from the tray. The pairing of the key light with food on that trial elevated the association between the key light and the food, convincing the pigeon to reinstate running to peck the key light on subsequent trials. The long box studies revealed that the pigeons were unable to control their key pecking that was so detrimental to eating the food, and this was the case despite their experience with eating the food on those trials when they did not engage in key pecking (Hearst & Jenkins, 1974).

The sign-tracking reflex is induced by mere experience with object-reward pairings. The discovery of the sign-tracking reflex provides us with a way of understanding the mysterious and poorly understood origins of the loss of self-control of drug-taking. At the heart of the drug addiction problem is the addict's inability to control their drug-taking, even though they insist that they are desperately trying to quit. The source of the disconnect between their action (taking the drug) and their intention (to abstain) may be due to their reflexive performance of the sign-tracking response. In other words, the mere presence of the cocktail glass, a powerful cue that signals the forthcoming rewarding effects of alcohol, may trigger the alcohol abuser to automatically and reflexively approach, contact, and bring the cocktail glass to their lips, as they drink the alcoholic beverage. All of this "just happens" without deciding to do it, without giving it a thought, and without any sense of conscious awareness of performing the action. In this way, the alcohol abuser drinks from the cocktail glass despite their every intention to decline the drink.

Chapter 10: The Misbehavior of Organisms

Professional animal trainers make their living by inducing animal subjects to perform specific tasks, as specified in written contractual agreements. The literature on the "misbehavior of organisms" describes instances where professional animal trainers failed to gain the cooperation of their animal subjects, and consequently, were unable to fulfill the contractual requirements, which was detrimental to their reputations as well as their pocketbooks. The earliest recorded observations of sign-tracking were described as the "misbehavior of organisms" by Keller and Marian Breland, professional animal trainers, who successfully trained hundreds of individual animals representing dozens of different species. They did so by requiring the animals to perform the desired task to receive a food reward (Breland & Breland, 1961, 1966). They enjoyed a sterling reputation for successfully training animals for television shows, movies, circus acts and Broadway plays. They did, however, experience some rather perplexing instances where things did not go according to plan. Their failures were carefully noted in a log, and before long an interesting pattern was discernible.

Misbehaving Raccoons:

In a typical example, a raccoon was initially trained to simply pick up a wooden coin for a food reward. This was quickly learned. Then, the raccoon was rewarded with food for picking up the wooden coin and carrying the wooden coin to the location of a small metal box. Then still an additional requirement was added to the response chain. The raccoon was required to pick up the coin, carry it to the box, then deposit the coin through a slot in the box. For doing so, the raccoon was promptly rewarded with a morsel of food. While initially things went well, with further training, the raccoon began to experience problems. The raccoon seemed unable to let go of the coins, spending several minutes handling two of them with their forepaws and "rubbing them together in a most miserly fashion". The raccoon often dipped the coin into the slot, only to pull them out again. In the end, the coins were chewed, licked, scratched, clawed, rubbed, and washed, but rarely deposited. Remarkably, the actions of the raccoons made it appear as though they were trying to clean a morsel of food, as raccoon are known to do, before eating. For interested readers, a brief video of misbehaving raccoons exhibiting sign-tracking behavior resulting in the loss of food rewards may be viewed at: https://www.youtube.com/watch?v=D52sQJEQI0Y.

Procedures conducive to misbehavior require the subject to relinquish a small object to obtain a food reward. Misbehavior develops after a period of successful performance of the required response, when formerly well-behaved subjects begin to persist in maintaining contact with the object and appear reluctant to let it go, even though these actions delayed, sometimes endlessly, the time of the delivery of the real food rewards. Thus, a prohibited response, maintaining contact with the small object, occurs and persists despite contingent loss of the food reward. The deterioration of performance occurs after a period of successful training with food rewards. Moreover, once the raccoon began to perform these feeding-appropriate responses, in lieu of relinquishing the coin, these responses became more of a problem with each passing day. In the end, the raccoon was receiving a very small percentage of the available food rewards.

The Brelands attempted to increase the raccoon's motivation for the food rewards by imposing a longer period of food deprivation prior to the daily training session. Increasing the raccoon's motivation to eat the food rewards only made matters worse. Ultimately the trainers were forced to give up and start over with a new raccoon subject, only to learn that the same thing happened with raccoon after raccoon. Other abandoned projected attempted similar training with pigs, rats, squirrel monkeys, chickens, turkeys, otters, porpoises, and whales.

The Brelands were thoroughly impressed by the robustness and species generality of the misbehavior effect. After their struggles to overcome it met with very little success, they eventually concluded that the behavior of their subjects came to be controlled by a deep-seated instinctive drive of unknown origin that gained in strength from their reward training procedures (Breland & Breland, 1966).

Irrational Behavior:

Sign-tracking is important because it provides us with a way of understanding how behavior can become irrational and defy free will. Consider the intention of the raccoon. The raccoon is hungry and very much interested in eating the morsel of food offered as the reward, but eventually, after many pairings of the coin and food, the raccoon's intention to devour those tasty morsels is seldom observed. Instead the raccoon's actions are those of sign-tracking. The disconnect between the raccoon's actions and the raccoon's intentions are not unlike those of the drug abuser, who intends to restrain drug-taking, but, instead, is unable to control the impulse to have yet another. In both cases, the subject is unable to suppress the action of consuming the object that predicts the reward.

Sign-tracking induces loss of self-control of action directed at the object that signals reward. This pretty much summarizes the essence of the problem of the drug addict. The drug addict is unable to control their drug-taking. They take the drug even when they are trying not to, and as in the case of sign-tracking, their problematic responding consists of action directed at the object that signals the reward. For example, addicts exhibit the symptoms of sign-tracking after they experience the object (cocktail glass) as a signal for reward (alcohol). In the presence of the cocktail glass they are drawn toward the glass and cannot resist reaching out and drinking from the glass. This suggests that the overlooked basis for the loss of self-control of drug-taking, the inability to terminate an ongoing drug use episode, is sign-tracking of drug-taking.

Chapter 11: Mistaken Identity

Scientists conducting behavioral studies in the analytical animal learning laboratory discovered a fascinating behavioral principal with profound implications for drug addiction. Their research revealed that when the subject is required to perform a voluntary response in order to obtain a reward, and, in addition, that voluntary response is directed at an object that predicts the reward, then sign-tracking responses develop that are also directed at the object cue, and these sign-tracking responses closely resemble the voluntary responses that induced them. Remarkably, this resemblance was so striking to the naked eye that specifically trained scientific observers could not tell them apart (Schwartz, 1975; Schwartz, et al., 1975; Schwartz & Williams, 1972). In addition, during such procedures, both response forms are directed at the same location, therefore, the induced sign-tracking responses had previously been mistaken for and added to the frequency counts of voluntary responses (for reviews, see Hearst & Jenkins, 1974; Schwartz & Gamzu, 1977). Thus, the experimental scientific evidence reveals that when the voluntary response is directed at an object that also provides a cue predictive of the reward, then sign-tracking responses develop and are masked to pass for voluntary responding. This masking effect is so effective that it remained concealed for many years and was revealed only by rigorous analytical experiments performed in the animal learning laboratory.

Drug-taking procedures in humans typically provide conditions conducive to this masking effect. That is, sign-tracking responses are induced that closely resemble voluntary drug-taking responses. Consider that the user is required to perform the voluntary drug-taking response to obtain the rewarding effects of the drug. In addition, note that the voluntary drug-taking response is directed at an object, the conduit employed to self-administer the drug, that predicts the rewarding effects of the drug. Under these conditions, the sign-tracking responses that develop are also directed at the conduit, the object cue that signals the drug reward, and these sign-tracking responses will closely resemble the voluntary drug-taking responses that induced them. In this way, sign-tracking responses will be masked, and therefore, prone to be misconstrued, due to errors of mistaken identity, as voluntary drug-taking responses.

Excessive Responding:

The discovery of mistaken identity shed light on several mysterious findings previously documented in the animal behavior literature. For many years, learning scientists were perplexed by what was presumed to be the excessive levels of voluntary goal-directed responding that developed when that responding was directed at the reward cue. Laboratory experiments were performed to examine this anomaly by exploring the effects of manipulating the location of the reward cue with respect to the location of the object that the subject was required to contact to obtain the reward. In other experiments, investigators examined the effects of varying the cue's positive correlation with the reward. These studies revealed that excessive voluntary-like responding was not observed in control conditions where the cue was located at a distance from the voluntary response target, or when the reward was equally likely to occur in the presence or the absence of the cue. In this way, investigators discovered that the excessive voluntary-like responding varied with precisely those conditions known to be conducive to the induction of sign-tracking responses.

Investigators concluded that the reward cue recruits sign-tracking responses that are indistinguishable from and additive with ongoing voluntary goal-directed responding (Hearst & Jenkins, 1974; Schwartz & Gamzu, 1977). In this way, scientists discovered that sign-tracking responses had long been mistaken for voluntary goal-directed responses, and the mistaken identity created the false impression that voluntary responding was being performed to excess (Tomie, et al., 1989). Note that the arrangements that produce this masking effect, bear a striking resemblance to those that are experienced by humans during bouts of excessive drug-taking (Tomie, 1995, 2018b).

This is because drug-taking in humans starts out as strictly a voluntary goal-directed response, performed to obtain the rewarding effects of the drug. The voluntary drug-taking response is directed at the object that serves as a conduit to assist in the self-administration of the drug. Due to repeated acts of voluntary drug-taking, where the conduit object is observed just before the drug's rewarding effects, the conduit object becomes a drug reward cue that elicits sign-tracking responses that are directed at the conduit object. This results in sign-tracking of drug-taking, which are reflexive and involuntary acts of drug-taking that are masked because they closely resemble the actions performed during voluntary acts of drug-taking. Due to mistaken identity, these reflexive acts of drug-taking are readily misconstrued as voluntary acts of drug-taking.

The discovery of sign-tracking opened the door to the intriguing possibility of mistaken identity. That is, under some circumstances, it is entirely possible that what appears to be a voluntary goal-directed response may, on closer inspection, turn out to be a reflexive Pavlovian cue-directed sign-tracking response. Note that even though sign-tracking may be induced during voluntary response training procedures, sign-tracking behavior is not performed to serve the goal-directed purpose of acquiring the food reward. Sign-tracking that is induced during voluntary response training procedures does not increase voluntary goal-directed behavior. Sign-tracking increases involuntary performance of voluntary-like responding. And, the conditions conducive to producing mistaken identity are provided when humans employ an object as a conduit to self-administer an abused drug (see Chapter 12). This suggests that prominent symptoms of drug addiction, including excessive drug-taking and loss of self-control of drug-taking, may be due to the development of sign-tracking.

Preposterous Imposters:

Preposterous imposters are created by the induction of sign-tracking of involuntary performance of voluntary-like responding that serve to thwart the goal directed intentions of the subject. This type of effect may bedevil the drug abuser who intends to refrain from drug use but is instead triggered to have yet another. In this way, voluntary responding directed at the reward cue may induce mistake-prone, erroneous, and unintended behavior that appears to be an intended voluntary response, but instead is a reflexive sign-tracking response. The unwelcome behavior is a well-disguised imposter. The actions are not voluntary, they are reflexive. Some examples of the sign-tracking response posing as an error-prone voluntary response include the feature-learning effect and the misbehavior effect.

The feature-learning effect provides an instance where the intrusion of sign-tracking resulted in error-prone responding during discriminative reward training procedures, that thwarted the subject's intention to provide accurate discrimination performance. In a typical study, the subject responds by touching the stimulus display. The S+ display is a red dot on a green background. The S- display is the same, except without the red dot. This is the feature-positive discrimination, which yields excellent choice accuracy. That is, the subjects respond on the S+ trials and the subjects withhold responding on the S- trials. The feature-negative procedure reverses the displays, so that the red dot, the distinguishing feature, is on the S-. Although the stimulus displays used in the two discrimination tasks are equally distinguishable from one another, subjects in the feature-negative condition make far more errors (Bitgood, et al., 1976; Norton, et al., 1971; Sainsbury, 1971).

Analysis of the location of responding supports a sign-tracking interpretation (Crowell & Bernhardt, 1979; Hearst & Jenkins, 1974). Feature-positive subjects tend to respond to the S+ display by touching the red dot, thereby recording a correct response, and earning the reward. Feature-negative subjects, on the other hand, tend to respond to their S+ display by touching the green background, also recording a correct response and earning the reward, but the pairing of the green display with the reward induces sign-tracking responses, leading to incorrect responding on S- trials. Some children expressed frustration upon performing the error, because they knew better, but responded automatically without thinking. This suggests that feature-negative errors were sign-tracking responses posing as voluntary responses. These sign-tracking responses are preposterous imposters that served to sabotage the intention of the subject, which was to produce accurate discrimination performance. Again, we have a case of mistaken identity where sign-tracking responses are indistinguishable from, and therefore recorded as voluntary goal-directed responses.

Misbehavior is another instance where reward training procedures induce mistake-prone, erroneous, and counterproductive responding that appears to be voluntary, but such responding is neither voluntary nor intended. The misbehaving raccoons are trained to perform a series of voluntary goal-directed responses to obtain a food reward. The well-trained raccoon is compliant and approaches the coin, picks up the coin, carries the coin to the bank, then deposits the coin into the slot, for which the raccoon is rewarded with a morsel of food. With continued training, the raccoon quickly becomes more and more proficient at approaching and contacting the coin and carrying the coin, but this apparently skilled performance appears to be due to sign-tracking.

The masquerade is over when the raccoon is unable to deposit the coin, as required to obtain the food reward. Instead, the raccoon dips the coin in the slot but cannot let it go, pulling it out to lick, gnaw, and rub the coin, behaving as though the coin were food. If the behavior of the raccoon was goal-directed and voluntary, then the hungry raccoon would deposit the coin, quickly and simply, to get the morsel of food and eat it. The raccoon appears to be exhibiting sign-tracking behavior, rather than voluntary goal-directed responding, which culminates in the raccoon's refusal to release the coin. These sign-tracking responses are preposterous imposters that served to sabotage the intention of the subject, which was to eat the food.

It should be noted that the misbehaving raccoons resemble drug abusers whose intention to refrain is thwarted by their triggered actions to have yet another. They are unable to stop themselves. They are repeatedly stymied by their inability to control themselves, as they are reflexively triggered to approach, contact, and "consume" the object that has been paired with the reward. When viewed through the lens of voluntary goal-directed behavior, the actions of the raccoons appear to be preposterous, if not outrageous. In a similar way, the actions of the drug abuser may also be a case of mistaken identity. In both cases, sign-tracking plays the role of the imposter, masquerading as voluntary and intended action. In both cases, the actions of the subject serve to thwart the intention of the subject, who is trying to refrain from performing the voluntary target-directed response, but, is unable to restrain the reflexive sign-tracking response.

Chapter 12: Conduits

Drug-taking procedures employed by humans typically involve the use of a small object that is employed as a conduit to assist in the self-administration of the drug (Tomie, 1995, 1996). During each act of drug-taking, the user handles and sees that small object, and all of this occurs in the moments in time just before the onset of the drug's rewarding effects. The conduit that is employed to self-administer the drug, therefore, predicts the rewarding effects of the drug. An analysis based on sign-tracking suggests that the conduit will become a trigger contributing to the loss of self-control of drug-taking. This idea will be further explored in the remainder of this chapter.

Drug-Taking in Humans:

The acquisition and maintenance of sign-tracking performance appears to be reliably induced by experience with pairings of an object and a reward; however, further experimental analysis revealed that more than mere object-reward pairings are required. Specifically, the object must also be differentially predictive of the reward, as revealed by studies where responding was neither acquired nor maintained, despite frequent object-reward pairings, when the food reward was equally like to occur in the absence of the object (Gamzu & Williams, 1973). Thus, in addition to object-reward pairings, sign-tracking requires a positive contingency or positive correlation or positive predictive relationship between the object and the reward. When, for example, the object and the reward are presented randomly with respect to one another, then the contingency between the object and the reward is zero, the correlation between the object and the reward is zero, and the predictive relationship between the object and the reward is zero. Under these conditions, when the object and the reward are presented randomly with respect to one another, sign-tracking performance is neither acquired nor maintained, despite occasional object-reward pairings that happen to occur by chance alone.

Thus, object-reward pairings induce sign-tracking to the extent that the reward is more likely to be delivered when the object has been presented, as compared to when the object has not been presented. In sign-tracking procedures, therefore, the key ingredient is the presentation of an object that predicts an elevated likelihood that the reward will be forthcoming.

An object that is differentially predictive of reward is the key ingredient that is essential to the development of sign-tracking responses, and this arrangement is widely observed in drug-taking procedures employed by humans. With respect to alcohol drinking, for example, alcohol's rewarding effects are more likely after drinking from the cocktail glass. For the marijuana user, the marijuana high is more likely after handling the bong, and for the cocaine user getting buzzed on cocaine is predicted by the presence of the pipe, while for the Oxycontin user, envelopment by opioid-induced quiescence is predicted by the appearance of the round pearl-colored disk-shaped tablet. In each of these drug-taking scenarios, the act of drug-taking provides the user with an object that predicts an elevated likelihood that the drug's rewarding effects will follow. Each of these drug-taking procedures, therefore, contains the key ingredient required to induce sign-tracking responses. Each time the drug-taking conduit is experienced, the drug's rewarding effects are more likely to follow as compared to when the drug-taking conduit has been absent. In this way, the drug-taking conduit becomes a drug-associated cue, encouraging the development of triggered acts of sign-tracking of reflexive, automatic, and involuntary drug-taking.

Morphine Intravenous (IV) Drip:

Suppose the drug is taken, but without using a conduit. The sign-tracking analysis predicts that under these conditions, loss of control will be less likely to develop. If object-reward pairings cause the loss of self-control of drug-taking, then the abuse liability of the drug should be reduced by taking the drug without using an object as a conduit to self-administer the drug. There is evidence suggesting that this is the case. For example, post-surgical pain management in hospitalized patients via intravenous (iv) morphine drip is associated with very low rates of patients subsequently developing addiction to opiates (Ballantyne & LaForge, 2007). The procedure typically provides for a solution of an opiate salt, usually morphine sulfate, to be continuously infused via a catheter tube taped to the patient's arm or hand. The low abuse liability of continuous intravenous (iv) morphine drip documented in post-surgical patients was one of several factors that encouraged the Food and Drug Administration (FDA) to approve prescription opiate pills for post-surgical pain management.

But, intravenous iv morphine drip procedures differ from prescription pain pill procedures in several important ways. When pain relief is obtained from a pill, the patient experiences a pairing of the object (pill) with the drug's rewarding effects (pain relief, euphoria, mood improvement) each time that the pill is taken. Repetitions of pairings of the pill with the rewarding effects of morphine may encourage the development of sign-tracking behaviors and the loss of control of drug-taking, as revealed by the development of automatic and reflexive pill-taking. With morphine intravenous iv drip, on the other hand, the patient does not experience object-reward pairings, because the clear plastic bag containing the morphine sulfate solution is continuously hanging from an intravenous iv rack that is typically located out-of-sight, behind the patient's bed.

Object-reward pairings may also contribute to the abuse liability of prescription pain pills in another way. Continuous infusions of morphine are more likely to produce a relatively constant steady-state concentration of plasma morphine levels, as compared to a time-table schedule of prescription pain pill medications, where plasma concentrations of the drug will rise sharply and peak shortly after taking the pill, and then slowly decline reaching a trough shortly before the time scheduled to take the next pill. Note that the scheduled pill-taking protocol provides especially effective pill-reward pairings because taking the pill is followed shortly thereafter by the peak of the cycle of the morphine-induced pain relief pattern. Though controlled-release opioids, such as OxyContin, have abuse-deterrent features intended to flatten the time-dependent variability of plasma concentrations, the concentrations ranges for OxyContin are nevertheless quite large relative to those documented with continuous morphine intravenous iv drip procedures. Thus, there is anecdotal evidence that drug-taking procedures that do not provide for object-reward pairings are less likely to induce loss of control of drug-taking, and this indicates that a feature of drug-taking procedures that may contribute to the abuse liability of the drug is object-reward pairings. These observations are consistent with an analysis based on sign-tracking.

Chapter 13: The Sign-Tracking Model

An analysis of drug addiction based on sign-tracking emphasizes the role of the tool used by humans as a conduit to aid in consuming the drug (Tomie, 1995, 1996). For example, through repetitions of voluntary drug-taking, the cocktail glass comes to signal an elevated likelihood of experiencing the rewarding effects of alcohol. In this way, repeated voluntary acts of alcohol drinking from the cocktail glass provide the user with repeated Pavlovian pairings, which are conducive to the induction of Pavlovian sign-tracking performance. The form or topography and the sequence of physical movements of sign-tracking performance of alcohol drinking will closely resemble the physical movements when performing acts of voluntary, intended alcohol drinking. Sign-tracking of drug-taking, therefore, is easily overlooked, and virtually invisible because sign-tracking of drug-taking looks very much like voluntary drug self-administration.

As alcohol use is repeated and loss of control of alcohol drinking begins to develop, voluntary acts of alcohol drinking will continue to take place as before. But now, in addition, due to the acquisition of sign-tracking, the drinker will absent-mindedly have a drink without intending to do it. This is not the same as deciding to have a drink. This is a triggered reflex. This is the first sign of the emergence of sign-tracking of alcohol drinking. Because the topography of the sign-tracking response closely resembles the topography of voluntary drug-taking, the user remains unconcerned, and may continue to drink excessively, having more than intended, but remain oblivious as to why.

As sign-tracking develops further, alcohol drinking will gradually become more reflexive, automatic, involuntary, mindless, and thoughtless, making alcohol drinking more difficult to stop. This is because, due to the strengthening of the association between the cocktail glass and alcohol's rewarding effects, the mere presence of the cocktail glass is now better able to trigger sign-tracking of alcohol drinking, resulting in reflexive drinking of the alcoholic beverage in the cocktail glass. Due to sign-tracking, an ongoing episode of alcohol drinking will be more difficult to stop, but the underlying cause of the actions of continued drinking will be overlooked. Having another drink will likely be passed off as a voluntary and intended action that is regrettable, but correctable, an unfortunate consequence of a bad decision. This overly optimistic view allows the abuser to cling to the mistaken belief that they are in control of their drug-taking when they are not. In this way, they remain blind to the erosion of their self-control as they continue to slide down the slippery slope into the pit of drug addiction.

The Origins of Sign-Tracking:

Figure 1 (see below) provides a flow chart depicting how each act of voluntary drug-taking (alcohol drinking in this example) provides the user with a Pavlovian CS-US pairing of the object (alcohol sipper, CS) with the reward (alcohol, US), leading to the development of sign-tracking conditioned response (CR) performance of alcohol sipper CS-directed approach, contact, and drinking responses. Each sign-tracking CR performance provides an additional CS-US pairing, leading to further strengthening of the CS-US association, and further strengthening of sign-tracking CR performance of reflexive alcohol drinking. Note that sign-tracking's positive feedback loop is further strengthened by alcohol's pharmacological effects which serve to increase sign-tracking CR performance in a dose-dependent fashion. Figure 1, using alcohol drinking as an example, illustrates how voluntary drug-taking brings about the development of sign-tracking performance of drug-taking.

Figure 1. The Sign-Tracking Model

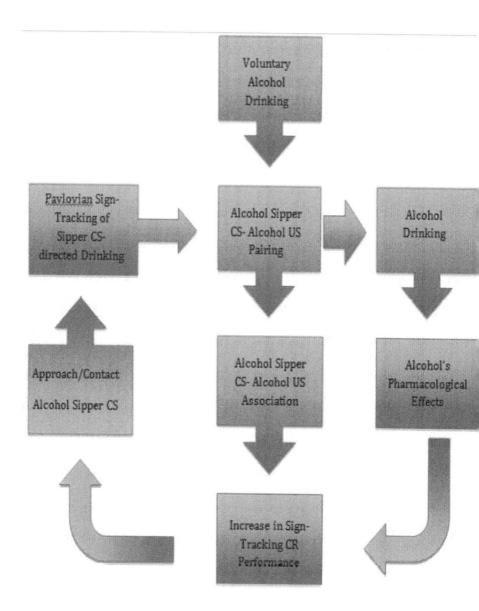

Figure 1: Voluntary alcohol drinking provides sipper-alcohol pairings that induce Pavlovian sign-tracking performance of alcohol drinking (Tomie & Sharma, 2013), resulting in additional sipper-alcohol pairings and still more reflexive alcohol drinking. Note that alcohol has the pharmacological effect of further increasing sign-tracking performance (Spoelder, et al., 2017; Tomie, et al., 1998).

An unintended role of the conduit, therefore, is to allow humans to self-administer drugs in a manner that is perfectly suited to the development of sign-tracking of drug-taking. Moreover, the conduit provides a common target at which both forms of drug-taking, voluntary intended drug-taking and reflexive sign-tracking of drug-taking, are directed, setting the stage for mistaken identity. As noted earlier, the form of the sign-tracking response is the same as the form of the voluntary response performed when the subject decides to have a drink. In both cases, the response form consists of approaching, contacting, and then consuming the beverage in the cocktail glass. Their shared common target, at the cocktail glass, serves to bring them together, merging them into a single unified stream of responding. In this way, the conduit triggers drug use that is excessive, that is, beyond that which was intended, and, at the same time, also serves to camouflage sign-tracking, creating a blind spot that allows the user to believe that their excessive use of drugs is by choice.

Thus, the user remains overconfident, unconcerned, and oblivious, even as drug-taking becomes increasingly difficult to control. The user is unable to see addiction coming because using a conduit to self-administer the drug serves to obscure the distinction between voluntary and reflexive drug use. This provides the opportunity for sign-tracking to develop, and slip by unnoticed, so that the user fails to recognize that they are not acting by choice but, instead, they are losing control of their drug-taking.

Drug Use Becomes Drug Abuse:

Sign-tracking models the loss of self-control of drug-taking, that transitions what starts out as voluntary, intended, social, recreational, well-managed drug use into the automatic, involuntary, reflexive, poorly-controlled, and unintended drug-taking of the drug abuser.

1. Sign-tracking responses are induced by experience with an object that predicts reward. This object-reward arrangement is typically observed during voluntary drug-taking procedures employed by humans. In this way, sign-tracking is induced by casual, recreational drug use.

2. The object-reward association induces the sign-tracking response, which is a Pavlovian acquired reflex that is automatically triggered when the subject is in the presence of the object that has been paired with the drug's rewarding effects.

3. The triggered and reflexive sign-tracking performances of drug-taking make it difficult for the subject to put an end to a bout of drug-taking, leading to binge-like episodes of excessive and poorly controlled drug-taking.

4. Each performance of sign-tracking of drug-taking provides the user with an additional experience with an object-reward pairing. This further strengthens the association between the object and the reward, which results in still additional triggered and reflexive sign-tracking performances of drug-taking.

5.   Sign-tracking performances of drug-taking responses that are triggered by object-reward pairings closely resemble the poorly controlled actions performed by users during acts of voluntary drug-taking. The resemblance is based on the forms or topographies of the responses and on their shared common target, the drug-taking implement. In this way, the sign-tracking response is camouflaged to resemble the voluntary drug-taking response that induced it.

6.   Due to mistaken identity, drug-taking due to sign-tracking responses are readily misconstrued by the subject as voluntary drug-taking responses, leading the subject to believe that they remain in control of their drug-taking when they are not.

7.   Sign-tracking responses merge with voluntary drug-taking responses to form a single unified stream of drug-taking responses that are performed to excess, relative to that which was intended. But, because the subject is oblivious to their diminished control of their drug-taking, they remain confident that quitting drugs is just a matter of deciding to do it.

The Hijacked Brain:

As sign-tracking of drug-taking develops, the user will find it increasingly more difficult to put an end to an ongoing bout of drug-taking. Drug-associated cues encourage the user to consume more drug than was originally intended, resulting in binge episodes of excessive and compulsive abuse of the drug. Continued, long-term drug abuse results in chronic exposure of the brain to elevated levels of the drug, a condition that is accompanied by chronic overactivation of DA activity in the NAC.

The brain adjusts to the increased DA in the system by reducing the number of DA receptors (Volkow, et al., 2010). This down-regulation of DA receptors in response to chronic overstimulation by abused drugs produces several of the most prominent and conspicuous behavioral symptoms expressed by the drug abuser. Reduced DA receptors are associated with the drug abuser's heightened expression of impulsive behaviors. Poor impulse control is notably evident when the drug abuser is unable to satisfy their need for the drug, as they are driven to escalating and compulsive self-administration of drugs (Volkow & Morales, 2015).

Anhedonia:

Reduced DA receptors in the mesolimbic DA reward pathways, in response to chronic drug abuse is also associated with a psychopathological state of "anhedonia", in which the drug abuser in unable to experience pleasure, not only in response to the drug but also in response to natural rewards like food, sex, and exercise, and social activities (Blum, et al., 1996). The word anhedonia is Greek for "without pleasure." The drug abuser experiences anhedonia from pushing their drug exposure envelope until further pushing has become futile. In the beginning they were able to gain more of the drug's effects by increasing the amount of drug taken, and in addition, by also reducing the intervals between successive drug doses. This enabled them to address their developing tolerance to the euphoric effects of the drug. In the end, they exhausted their DA system, which was no longer able to respond to DA release. Due to the exhaustion of their DA system, the brain of the drug abuser is no longer able to create the emotional state of reward or pleasure.

In retrospect, this did not happen in an instant. This was a long time in the making. For many weeks or months, as their drug-taking escalated, the drug abuser was gradually getting boxed into a corner, exhibiting progressively less interest in their formerly favorite things and activities. Their favorites foods were ignored, their libido diminished, and keeping up with their favorite sports teams or music groups was long forgotten. They derived no pleasure from their accomplishments in athletics, academics, or work. Their work habits deteriorated as their career ambitions plummeted, along with their standards of grooming, dress, and personal hygiene. They spent less time with family, and the only remaining survivors in their circle of friends are those who share their affection for their drug of choice. Admittedly, this is not necessarily unusual or abnormal, as most people will, at some point in their life, lose interest in things or activities that used to excite them. Anhedonia, however, takes this loss to its extreme limits. It becomes impossible for the drug abuser to draw enjoyment from any of the things that once elicited excitement. Ironically, the drug abuser, the formerly self-proclaimed hedonist, ends up unable to experience pleasure.

Anhedonia is a devastating psychopathological disorder that is prominent in the diagnosis of Major Depressive Disorder (MDD), which is also called Melancholia (Destoop, et al., 2019). Those afflicted find themselves in a world that offers no rewards or pleasures or even temporary moments of respite from overwhelming feelings of depression, dysphoria, hopelessness, and despair (Heshmati & Russo,

2015), giving rise to the elevated incidence of suicide among patients diagnosed with MDD (Grunebaum, et al., 2004). It should come as no surprise (Case & Deaton, 2020; Cheatle, 2011; Woolf & Schoomaker, 1996) that the geographical distribution of recent addiction-related overdose deaths coincides remarkably with the geographical distribution of recent deaths by suicide (Congdon, 2019; Wilt, et al., 2019). The remarkable congruence between the maps of their geographical distributions over time suggests a far more sinister and disturbing interpretation of the ongoing epidemic of drug overdose deaths.

Chapter 14: Alcohol Drinking Styles

Alcohol drinking styles that are conducive to the development of sign-tracking are differentially associated with the loss of control of alcohol drinking in humans. For example, the practice of drinking alcoholic beverages only from specialized alcohol-only drinking containers, such as glassware, mugs, or steins, has been associated with elevated rates of loss of self-control of alcohol drinking, as revealed by documented incidents of problem drinking (public intoxication, disorderly conduct, assault, driving while intoxicated or impaired, domestic violence, etc.) noted in the public record. This evidence is based on regional differences across Europe in alcohol drinking styles that are associated with regional differences in problem drinking rates.

Cultural anthropologists have found higher rates of problem drinking in Northern Europe, as compared to Mediterranean Europe, even though the per capita consumption of alcohol in those regions is comparable (de Lint, 1973; Heath, 1987). While many cultural aspects of alcohol drinking may contribute to these regional disparities in problem drinking rates, it should be noted that the types of drinking containers used to consume alcoholic beverages differ across regions, with specialized alcohol-only drinking containers more generally employed in Northern Europe than in Southern Europe (Levin, 1990), . These specialized alcohol drinking containers include high refraction lead crystal glasses, tumblers, stemware, goblets, and flutes, as well as ornate metallic or ceramic mugs and steins. Using specialized glassware or ornate mugs to consume alcoholic beverages is more broadly practiced in northern Europe than southern Europe (Levin, 1990), and the prevalence of poorly controlled binge drinking varies across Europe in this same way (de Lint, 1973; Heath, 1987; Levin, 1990). Note that the sign-tracking hypothesis predicts that using specialized alcohol-only drinking containers will enhance their predictive relationship to alcohol's rewarding effects, leading to sign-tracking and elevated incidents of problem drinking. .

Specialized vs Common Glassware:

An analysis based on sign-tracking, for example, suggests that the practice of specializing glassware exclusively for consuming alcoholic beverages will enhance the positive contingency between the item of specialized glassware and the alcohol reward. This is because the specialized glassware is used solely and exclusively for the purpose of consuming alcoholic beverages. The specialized glassware, therefore, is never used and, in addition, has never previously been used, to drink a non-alcoholic beverage, such as milk or water or lemonade. Thus, alcohol's rewarding effects are more likely to follow when the specialized glassware has been observed, as compared to when the specialized glassware has not been observed. The specialized glassware, therefore, is positively predictive of alcohol's rewarding effects, and, consequently the specialized glassware will serve as a more effective trigger eliciting reflexive and involuntary acts of sign-tracking of alcohol drinking. This will play out in the tavern when the user is the presence of the distinctive specialized glassware. The user will find themselves unable to restrain having another, despite the intention to limit their intake. In this way sign-tracking, triggered by and directed at the specialized glassware, will make it more difficult to put an end to an ongoing episode of alcohol drinking, resulting in elevated rates of problem drinking.

For purposes of comparison, consider the effects on the rate of problem drinking of a different alcohol drinking style, where the same common everyday drinking glasses and cups are used to consume non-alcoholic beverages as well as alcoholic beverages. This is a drinking style that is typical of Italy and other countries of Mediterranean Europe, where in homes and in cafes and restaurants, common everyday table glasses and cups are often used to consume alcoholic beverages. Note that these same common everyday table glasses and cups are used in their daily lives by most individuals to consume non-alcoholic beverages, including water, milk, soda, fruit juice, etc. And, in addition, these glasses and cups have been used daily in this way for many years, dating back to childhood.

The common glassware drinking style will lead to less association between the common glassware and alcohol's reward effects because the common glassware has also often been used to drink non-alcoholic beverages. When this happens, the common glassware is observed during the course of drinking, but alcohol's rewarding effects do not follow. Thus, an analysis based on sign-tracking predicts that the common glassware drinking style will produce a lower positive contingency between the common glassware and alcohol's rewarding effects. It follows, therefore, that poorly controlled problem drinking is less likely to develop when the glassware or cup is employed for consuming non-alcoholic as well as alcoholic beverages. The observed regional differences between problem drinking rates and the use of specialized as compared to common glassware are consistent with the hypothesis that sign-tracking contributes to the loss of control of alcohol drinking in humans.

Does sign-tracking contribute to the abuse liability of other addictive drugs, including, for example, marijuana, tobacco, cocaine, amphetamines, or opiates? The development of sign-tracking is induced by voluntary drug-taking procedures that provide experience with an object that predicts an elevated likelihood that the drug's rewarding effects will follow. This positive predictive relationship is particularly likely to be observed when that object is explicitly specialized to be employed exclusively as a conduit for the sole purpose of drug self-administration. Thus, conditions conducive to the development of sign-tracking are provided when humans endeavor to consume abused drugs with the assistance of a tool employed as a conduit to self-administer the drug.

A drug-taking tool is an implement designed to deliver the drug to the brain quickly and efficiently, while also allowing the user to control their exposure to the dose-related effects of the drug. There are numerous examples of drug-taking tools of this sort. For example, marijuana or tobacco is typically consumed by burning the leaves or the high-resin bud. The smoke is inhaled, using a bong or pipe or Juul pod or rolling papers as a funnel to deliver the smoke to the lungs. Black tar heroin or white heroin powder is heated until liquified then drawn into the barrel of a hypodermic syringe where it is diluted with the user's blood, then injected into a vein.

Powdered cocaine hydrochloride salt is typically snorted into a nostril using a narrow straw, tube or tooter. Crystalline cocaine in the form of a crack rock or free-base cocaine powder is ignited by flame, then the vapors are inhaled through the stem of a pipe. Synthetic opioid pain medications, such as OxyContin are typically consumed orally. Organic chemists refined the opiate base, typically starting with morphine or codeine, which were then pressed into individual compact pills, to be swallowed by the user to obtain a precisely metered dose of pain relief over a more extended interval of time. It was soon discovered that chewing an OxyContin tablet — or crushing one and snorting the powder, or injecting it with a needle — produced an instant high as powerful as heroin and this has led to widespread abuse of synthetic opioid pain pills.

Each of these drug-taking implements is specialized to fulfill the intended application of drug-taking. Moreover, it seems unlikely that these tools were repurposed from other uses. The drug-taking implement, therefore, signals an elevated likelihood that the rewarding effects of the drug will follow, relative to when the drug-taking implement has not been observed (Tomie, 1995), and is likely to be highly predictive of the drug's rewarding effects. In this respect these specialized drug-taking implements, the marijuana bong, the Juul pod, the hypodermic syringe, the crack pipe, the medication pill, share much in common with specialized alcohol-only drinking glassware, in that they are all highly likely to quickly become associated with the drug's rewarding effects. For this reason, they may quickly develop the tendency to trigger reflexive and involuntary acts of drug-taking. In doing so, they serve to encourage binge-like bouts of excessive and poorly controlled drug-taking, making it more difficult to put an end to an ongoing episode of drug-taking.

Broad vs Narrow Repertoire:

Drinkers of alcoholic beverages may differ in their drinking style based on the number of different types of alcohol drinking containers they employ when consuming an alcoholic beverage. For example, suppose two drinkers consume alcohol and, to simplify matters both individuals drink only beer, but they differ in the range of their beer drinking repertoires. One user drinks beer only from a 12-ounce amber bottle. This individual has a very narrow drinking repertoire. For comparison purposes, another individual also drinks only beer, but is less particular, so he drinks beer from a wide range of alcoholic beverage containers. For example, this individual may drink his favorite beer from an amber bottle on Monday, from a blue Dixie cup on Tuesday, from an ornate metal mug on Wednesday, from a glass stein on Wednesday, from an aluminum can on Friday, and so forth. This individual has a broader beer drinking repertoire.

An analysis based on sign-tracking predicts that, for any given number of drinks consumed, the individual with the broader drinking repertoire will be less likely to exhibit poorly controlled problem drinking. The prediction may seem puzzling, because the person with the broad drinking repertoire will have experienced many different drinking containers paired with alcohol's rewarding effects. But a contingency analysis reveals that for the broad repertoire the association between each specific drinking container and alcohol's rewarding effects will continually remain weak. This is because each specific drinking container that is absent when alcohol is consumed will experience a reduction in their positive contingency relationship with alcohol's rewarding effect. This is because alcohol reward was experienced even though that specific container was absent, and this serves to reduce the event co-variation between that container and alcohol's rewarding effects. Thus, on each day, the container-alcohol association is strengthened only for the container employed to drink alcohol on that day, while, at the same time, the container-alcohol association is diminished for each of the absent containers. The broader the range of the drinking repertoire, the more likely that any specific container will be absent when alcohol is consumed.

An analysis based on sign-tracking predicts that individuals who adopt the broad repertoire drinking style will develop weak alcohol reward associations to many alcohol drinking containers, and strong alcohol reward associations to none of them. This individual will less likely be triggered by any of their many alcohol drinking containers to perform sign-tracking of alcohol drinking. On the other hand, the individual who drinks beer only from the same amber beer bottle every day will develop a strong association between alcohol reward and their amber beer bottle. This individual is far more likely to be triggered by their amber beer bottle to perform sign-tracking responses, resulting in automatic and reflexive acts of drug-taking that will make it more difficult to put an end to an alcohol drinking episode.

The range of the alcohol drinking repertoire varies considerably across age groups and, in addition, may change dramatically across the life span. The broad drinking repertoire is an alcohol drinking style that is most prevalent among younger individuals, and particularly among those who are in the earliest stages of initiating alcohol use. During this time, individuals are unlikely to have settled into a habitual pattern of alcohol use and are unlikely to have developed a strong preference for any favorite alcoholic beverage, served only in a specific way. It is during this period of young adulthood, 18-25 years old, that peak alcohol consumption during the lifespan is typically noted (Labouvie, e al., 1997), but most of these individuals do not subsequently go on to develop a pattern of problem drinking in adulthood (Bates & Labouvie, 1997; White, et al., 2005).

The absence of evidence indicating a stronger connection between their high levels of alcohol drinking in their youth, and their subsequent vulnerability to problem drinking later in life, may be due to their tendency in their younger years to forage broadly while they rummage through an extensive list of possible alcoholic beverage candidates. Going forward, they carry their reduced contingency values to their many drinking containers, reducing the chances of being triggered to perform sign-tracking of alcohol drinking. This allows

them to be effectively immunized against developing sign-tracking of poorly controlled alcohol drinking later in life.

Evidence from prospective longitudinal studies indicate that during the life span the preferred style of alcohol drinking may systematically change, and often does so in a predictable way. Across the years, the range of the alcohol drinking repertoire typically becomes narrower, and the systematic narrowing of the drinking repertoire is often associated with the subsequent development of problem drinking (Cottler, et al., 1995; Jellinek, 1960; McCreary, 2002). Thus, the narrowing of the drinking repertoire has been broadly recognized as an age-related risk factor for the development of alcohol abuse. As time moves forward, and the drinking repertoire becomes increasingly narrow, alcohol is eventually consumed only in the form of a favorite alcoholic beverage that is prepared and served only in a very specific way. Thus, a favorite alcoholic beverage is eventually consumed repeatedly and habitually in the same place and from the same type of specialized alcohol drinking glassware.

In the details of their medical records related to their clinical case studies, addiction nosologists have documented the consistent and predictable longitudinal progression into alcoholism. While their data clearly reveal an association between the narrowing of the repertoire and problem drinking, this evidence is admittedly anecdotal rather than experimental, and, therefore, it remains unclear which is the "cause" and which is the "effect". The sign-tracking analysis presumes that the narrowing of the drinking repertoire is the cause of the loss of control of alcohol drinking, and this is clearly the interpretation favored by the addiction nosologists. However, it is entirely possible that the cause-effect arrow points in the other direction. That is, perhaps it is the loss of control of alcohol drinking that causes the subsequent narrowing of the drinking repertoire.

According to this view, as loss of control of alcohol drinking develops, each episode of uncontrollable alcohol drinking sets the stage for the next one. The cocktail glass that was used to consume the last drink of the previous night's binge will likely still be present and readily available to be used the next day when drinking will resume. In this way, the narrowing of the drinking repertoire is a consequence of the high frequency of rapidly sequenced episodes of poorly controlled drinking. Thus, the habit of drinking more and more exclusively from a specific cocktail glass may be caused by the habitual daily pattern of excessive alcohol drinking, rather than the other way around. More rigorous analysis of the association between the habit of beverage exclusivity and the loss of control of alcohol drinking will require careful recording of data in prospective longitudinal studies that include highly detailed information regarding the specific alcohol drinking implements employed by each specific individual prior to and after the transition from alcohol use into alcohol abuse.

A long-time associate has recently developed the habit of drinking too much. He drinks alcohol almost every day, typically after work, while seated at the bar, in his favorite cocktail lounge, where he has long been a regular. His favorite drink is a dry martini, extra dry, with a twist, two olives, and an onion. This drink is always served "up" and always prepared in a very specific way, using specific brands of gin and dry vermouth. The beverage is then poured into a serrated lead crystal tumbler. Day after day, time after time, the same exact thing. While this does simplify the ordering of drinks (i.e., "I'll have the usual."), the narrow drinking repertoire is associated with elevated rates of problem drinking, and this may be the case because this style of alcohol drinking favors the development of sign-tracking.

The presence of the lead crystal tumbler reliably signals an elevated likelihood that alcohol reward is on the way, while the absence of the lead crystal tumbler signals that alcohol reward is unlikely. The lead crystal tumbler, therefore, is an excellent signal that is highly predictive of alcohol's rewarding effects. Due to its elevated cue value, the lead crystal tumbler will be an effective trigger unleashing sign-tracking, resulting in reflexive acts of automatic and unintended alcohol drinking. Due to its tendency to promote the development of sign-tracking, the narrow drinking repertoire will be associated with binge episodes of poorly controlled alcohol drinking, that will contribute to elevated rates of problem drinking. Thus, an analysis based on sign-tracking predicts that the tendency to drink alcohol exclusively in a very particular way is highly likely to induce poorly controlled binge-like episodes of glassware-triggered alcohol drinking, making it more difficult to put an end to an ongoing alcohol drinking episode.

Breaking Old Habits:

What are the therapeutic implications of sign-tracking? The evidence relating styles of alcohol drinking to the loss of self-control of alcohol drinking suggests that the problem drinker with the narrow drinking repertoire should make immediate alterations in the way that they drink. They should abandon the habit of drinking their favorite alcoholic beverage from their favorite glassware, and, instead, they should drink their favorite alcoholic beverage only from containers never before used to consume an alcoholic beverage. This will serve to broaden their drinking repertoire. Using a soup mug or a plastic infant cup, or other common glassware, to drink their martini cocktail should reduce triggered acts of alcohol drinking, making it more likely that an episode of alcohol drinking will be discontinued when stopping is intended. In addition, they should adopt the practice of drinking only non-alcoholic beverages, such as milk, fruit juice, etc., from their favorite cocktail glass. This will serve to erode the positive contingency between the favorite cocktail glass and alcohol's rewarding effects, reducing sign-tracking and the incidence of poorly controlled drinking.

There are also implications of sign-tracking for retarding the development of the loss of control of alcohol drinking. For example, the data suggest that an effective strategy would be to use alcohol glassware but only to consume non-alcoholic beverages. This should be done for many years prior to the initiation of alcohol drinking later in life. This practice is analogous to the signal pre-exposure procedures in the Pavlovian conditioning laboratory (Lubow & Moore, 1959), where the effect is to retard the acquisition of the Pavlovian sign-tracking response (Sparber, et al., 1991; Tranberg & Rilling, 1978). The effectiveness of this procedures is consistent with the finding that the common glassware drinking style is associated with lower levels of problem drinking in Europe.

Sipper-Alcohol Contingency Effects in Animals:

In humans, alcohol drinking is directly related to the positive contingency between alcohol's rewarding effects and the alcohol glassware from which alcohol is consumed. Are animals similarly affected? That is, do animals consume more alcohol when in the presence of an alcohol sipper tube that is more highly predictive of alcohol reward? Put another way, are there data from animals indicating that procedures conducive to the development of sign-tracking induce more alcohol drinking? In these studies of voluntary alcohol self-administration in rats, a laboratory rat is provided with the opportunity to drink an alcohol solution from a sipper tube. Note that the sipper tube is the tool employed as a conduit to assist in the drinking of the alcoholic beverage. Note also that the alcohol solution, and its rewarding effects, are unavailable when the sipper tube is absent. The positive contingency between the sipper tube and the alcohol reward will elicit sign-tracking performance of sipper-directed alcohol drinking, which will add to voluntary alcohol drinking, resulting in elevated levels of alcohol intake. Studies that vary the contingency between the sipper and alcohol reveal that alcohol intake is elevated when the event co-variation contingency between the sipper and alcohol is higher (Tomie, et al., 2003, 2005, 2006).

The positive contingency between the sipper and the alcohol varies directly as a function of the ratio of the duration of the non-sipper (i.e., sipper retraction) periods relative to the duration of the sipper presentation (i.e., sipper insertion) periods (Balsam & Gibbon, 1988;

Gallistel & Gibbon, 2000; Jenkins, et al., 1981). Intermittent sipper procedures improve the co-variation between the sipper and the alcohol by increasing the amount of time during the daily drinking session that the sipper and the alcohol are both absent, improving their co-variation. Therefore, an analysis based on sign-tracking predicts that lengthening the duration of the periods of time during the daily drinking session that the sipper is retracted from the drinking chamber will have the effect of elevating sign-tracking of alcohol drinking (Tomie, et al., 2003a, 2003b; 2005).

An intermittent schedule of availability of the alcohol sipper (Intermittent Sipper procedure) provides for repeated insertions and retractions of the alcohol sipper such that the alcohol sipper is removed from the drinking chamber during most of the drinking session. In a Continuous Sipper procedure, fixed position alcohol drinking tubes provide for continuous availability of the alcohol sipper during the entire duration of the drinking session. Remarkably, it has been reported in several studies that the Intermittent Sipper procedure induced more total alcohol intake per session than the Continuous Sipper procedure, even though the Intermittent Sipper procedure provided the rats with far less time to drink alcohol from the sipper, which was retracted for the majority of the daily drinking session (Tomie, et al., 2005, 2006).

Similar effects of intermittent sipper procedures versus continuous sipper procedures have been reported in studies of home cage alcohol drinking. Rats provided with continuous access to the alcohol sipper in their home cage drink less alcohol per day than rats deprived of access to the alcohol sipper, and consequently, access to the alcohol solution, on some of the days (Brancato, et al., 2016; Carnicella, et al., 2014; Loi et al., 2010; Peris, et al., 2015; Sabino, et al., 2013; Simms, et al., 2008, 2013). This effect has also been reported in mice (Melendez, 2011). This suggests that the effect of the positive sipper-alcohol contingency on the elevation of daily levels of alcohol intake are evident across a broad range of alcohol drinking procedures.

Chapter 15: The Drug-Taking Ritual

Drug-taking does not take place at random times, in random locations, or in the presence of a random assortment of people. When, where and with whom drug-taking takes place may vary greatly from one person to the next, but for any specific individual, one thing is clear. When it comes to drug-taking, we are creatures of habit. We tend to repeatedly self-administer the drug around the same time of day, in a favored drug-taking location, and in the company of the same group of friends who share in common a desire to use our drug of choice. Just to be clear, this is not required of us, but this is how it seems to work out. And, it is not unusual for things to go even further down this narrow path, to the point where drug-taking is ritualized (Falk, 1986).

As drug-taking becomes progressively more repetitive and habitual, the settings in which drug-taking take place and the actions performed in taking the drug become more and more highly uniform, to the point of becoming ritualized. Tiffany (1990) notes that as drug-taking becomes more routine, a well-practiced habit, the actions performed when taking the drug become a rigid and automatic robotic-like performance, resembling an automatic action schemata. A drug-taking ritual is a sequence of activities involving gestures, words, and objects, performed in a sequestered place, and performed according to a set sequence. Drug-taking is ritualistic when the act of drug-taking follows a narrow and set sequence of actions: collecting the drug itself, assembling the drug-use tools, preparing the drug, loading the drug into the tool, and self-administering the drug. In the extreme, a drug-taking ritual is a ceremonial and religious-like act of worship that serves to prepare the user to receive the blessing (Grund, 1993).

Ritualized Drug-Taking:

The opioid injection ritual was described in vivid detail by Jerry Stahl: "This was a pattern: I clenched that sleeve in my teeth and softly, lovingly, secretly, eased the needle into my throbbing vein, watched with awe and reverence as the blood from my own body flowed back and up the blessed needle. Then I pressed won gently, shoved the poppy nectar, now stained red, slow as glacial erosion into my bloodstream and off on its holy journey north to heart and onward, upward to the waiting portals of my brain, where the high priest waited, welcoming the latest flagrant sacrifice to the God of Solitude, the God of Strangeness, the God of Sweet and Terrifying and Secret Ecstasy."

(*Permanent Midnight. A Memoir*, pages 138-139). New York, NY: Warner Books.

It is a matter of public lore, captured in song and verse. Drug addicts have meticulously detailed the salacious anticipation that accompanies the performance of the well-learned ritual preceding drug-taking. This suggests that addicts are as hooked on the rituals of getting high as they are on the rush itself. Etta James describes her habit of going for a double dose of injected heroin:

"I liked seeing the needle stuck in the vein between hits. The danger was thrilling. Shooting was thrilling. And then there's the cotton, the sifter, the spoon, the cooking, the needle, the penetration. The self-infliction. The ritual." *(Rage to Survive*, page 108).

The drug-taking ritual is an extreme example of a very narrow repertoire, and, as such, the ritual use of drugs should be highly conducive to the development of sign-tracking and then, to the subsequent loss of self-control of drug-taking. It comes as no surprise that ritual use of drugs is widely regarded as extremely dangerous, and as the most highly addictive form of drug-taking (Gray, 2014). Loss of control of drug-taking occurs very rapidly, even when relatively low doses of the drug are taken, and ritual drug users are particularly likely to suffer recurring relapses due to their extreme vulnerability to triggered acts of automatic drug-taking set in motion by drug-associated cues (White, 1996).

Numerous scientific reports reveal that situational stimuli that are present at the time that the drug is consumed become associated with the drug's euphoric effects (Rohsenow, et al., 1994; Sherman, et al., 1989). These drug-associated cues will come to elicit conditioned euphoric reactions which are additive with the euphoria induced by the drug itself. Thus, the drug-taking ritual is conducive to producing extremely intense euphoric reactions due to the summation of drug-induced euphoria added to the conditioned euphoria elicited by the cues associated with the ritual (Di Ciano & Everitt, 2004). The cues associated with the performance of the drug-taking ritual formalize the anticipatory reception of the arrival of the drug. Ritual cues trigger powerful emotional states described as aching anticipation and nervous arousal, and waves of desire for the drug's effects (Monti, et al., 1987).

Rituals of Behavioral Addictions:

Drug addiction is certainly the most widely recognized form of the more general behavioral disorder of "addiction". Recently, the term addiction has been applied to a much broader range of habitual behaviors, referred to as behavioral addictions or impulse control disorders, or reward non-substance-related addictions. Behavioral addictions share many of the general characteristics that we see with drug addiction, including excessive responding, poorly controlled responding, and the persistence of responding despite negative consequences. The most prevalent forms of behavioral addictions include gambling, internet gaming, shopping, sex, pornography, hoarding, food, and use of smart phone, and use of social media. While behavioral addictions have been proposed as a new class, in *Diagnostic and Statistical Manual of Mental Disorders, Fifth Edition* (DSM-5), only gambling addiction was formally recognized as a behavioral addiction, although internet gaming addiction was included in the Appendix as a condition for further study.

Behavioral addictions are more difficult to study than are drug addictions. In the case of an abused drug the investigator has available for study a tangible physical entity, the drug molecule, that can be tagged and traced, in order to document its specific point of entry into the brain and from there, where it goes and what it does … its pathways, binding sites, and metabolic fate. Behavioral addictions, on the other hand, do not provide a tangible physical entity that can be precisely traced and whose journey and metabolism can be studied and evaluated.

Another difference is that abused drugs are readily studied using animal models. Much of what we know about drug addiction comes to us from the study of the effects of abused drugs on the behavior and the brain functioning of animal subjects. Behavioral addictions, on the other hand, such as internet addiction or shopping addiction or smart phone addiction, are more difficult to model with animals, largely because in animals these behaviors typically do not exist. Thus, there are few published scientific experimental reports that document behavioral addictions in animals, and there are virtually no systematic studies that have explored the relationship between sign-tracking and behavioral addictions in animals.

The lone exception is gambling addiction, which has been modeled in experiments using animal subjects, and, in addition, has been explored for the possible relevance of sign-tracking. Gambling was more readily accepted by scientists as a behavioral addiction because at the time there were already numerous published scientific studies of gambling addiction or compulsive gambling disorder. These studies showed that in humans gambling activates similar parts of the brain, including the ascending mesolimbic DA pathway projection to NAC, as are activated by abused drugs (Potenza et al., 2003).

More recently, behavioral studies of gambling revealed many interesting parallels between gambling behavior in humans and addictive behaviors in animals, and, in some case, effects suggest a relationship to sign-tracking. For example, there is evidence that sign-tracking and attentional bias in human gamblers share much in common. For example, gamblers displayed greater attentional bias and fixed their gaze for longer periods of time on gambling-related cues (Hudson, et al., 2016; McCusker & Gettings, 1997; McGrath, et al., 2018). Moreover, high-risk gamblers show greater sustained attention toward gambling cues than low-risk gamblers (Hudson, et al., 2016), and gamblers maintain their gaze longer on cues that match their preferred form of gambling (McGrath, et al., 2018). Problematic gamblers also visually fixate their gaze and spend more time looking at gambling-related cues than non-gamblers, suggesting that they automatically detect and have difficulty disengaging from gambling-related stimuli (Brevers, et al., 2011).

The array of cues in the gambling environment, the flashing lights and the symphony of sounds of gaming chips, tumbling dice, spinning roulette wheels, and whirling slot machines, not only strengthen the eliciting of attentional bias, but these gambling-related cues also possess the ability to elicit craving and induce urges to gamble (Kushner, et al., 2008, Park, et al., 2015; Potenza, et al. 2003; Wulfert, et al., 2009). Most significantly, the finding that the persistence of sign-tracking is enhanced by reward uncertainty (Anselme, et al., 2013), in much the same way that the conditioned attractiveness of the pulsating lights and symphony of sounds of the casino contribute to the persistence of attentional bias and compulsive gambling disorder in humans (Anselme, 2018; Robinson & Anselme, 2019).

While technology has provided an unprecedented expansion in the number of different forms of expression of behavioral addictions, and many of the technology-related behavioral addictions appear to be amenable to an analysis based on sign-tracking, there remains, outside of gambling, no published studies documenting an effect of sign-tracking procedures, relative to control procedures, on the acquisition and maintenance of behavioral addictions. Thus, the evidence that sign-tracking plays a role in the pathological usage of smart phones, social media, internet gaming, texting, etc., remains largely suggestive and anecdotal.

Smart Phone Rituals:

Drug addiction shares a number of characteristics with other loss-of-self-control disorders including a number of more recently emerging behavioral addictions, particularly technology related disorders, such as compulsive usage of the smart phone, social media, texting, internet gaming, online shopping, photo-sharing, tweeting, etc. Are you addicted to your smart phone? Does the "ding" of your smart phone improve your mood? Is the "ding" of your smart phone so welcome and rewarding that you feel compelled to immediately pick up the phone to see who is there. You must know, who is "dinging" you and why? Do you respond to the "ding" even while engaged in other important activities, such as driving a car or writing a paper or taking lecture notes? Have you ever misplaced your smart phone, or have you ever lost it, even for a short period of time? Do you recall feeling anxious or uncomfortable, not having your smart phone with you? Are you at all concerned that you may be addicted to your smart phone?

I was watching a group of teenagers sitting around a table, each staring at the screen of their smart phone, texting each other, rather than talking to each other. They were thumbing and reading, then thumbing some more. One cannot help but wonder ... I mean, their behavior has that quality of excessiveness and single-minded obsessiveness that we so often see with drug abusers. And, in addition, consistent with an analysis based on sign-tracking, their obsession revolves around a relatively small object, the smart phone, that is closely and repeatedly paired with the rewarding "ding". This object-reward pairing is a fundamental aspect of smart phone use, and fits in quite well with sign-tracking, lending support to the idea that responding to their smart phone is an automatic and involuntary reflex. Subjects respond immediately to the "ding" by approaching their phone, and then picking up their phone, and then consuming the information on the screen, then quickly firing off a response. Then, they place the phone near at hand, while waiting for the next "ding". Their obsession with their smart phone is so distracting that they interact very little, if at all, with their friends seated at their table. And, from what I can see, this behavior is not an isolated aberration. This can go on during much of the day, day after day, at home, at school, and everywhere in between. These teenagers appear, arguably, to be addicted to their smart phones.

It used to be, several years ago, when I walked up to the door of my lecture hall, I would see several small clusters of students, standing around, waiting for the start of the lecture, chit-chatting among themselves. Things have changed, considerably. Now what I am likely to encounter is a line of solitary, individual students, each standing or sitting, back to the wall, lining the entry alcove to the lecture hall doors, each of them doing the same thing, busily thumbing away on their smart phone. None of these students is talking face-to-face with another student. I can only surmise that interacting with their smart phone is their favorite and most rewarding activity. Are they addicted to their smart phone? Can they decide to stop? Can they ignore the next "ding", putting an end to an ongoing bout of interacting with their cell phone? Will they turn off their phones and listen to my lecture?

Chapter 16: The Addictive Personality

The long-standing and generally accepted, historical point of view was that mere exposure to an addictive drug could place virtually anyone at risk for developing a substance use disorder (Bejerot, 1972). More recently, however, scientists have focused on the individual differences that make certain individual more at risk than others. People are certainly not equally prone to becoming addicted, and this suggests the intriguing possibility of identifying a pre-existing behavioral trait that constitutes a marker of vulnerability to drug addiction (Cofresi, et al., 2019; Flagel, et al., 2009; Tunstall & Kearns, 2014).

Individuals differ greatly from one another in their vulnerability to drug addiction, and in a similar fashion, individuals also differ greatly from one another in their tendency to exhibit sign-tracking performance. Recently, addiction scientists have found that the variations in these two behavioral tendencies co-vary within an individual subject. That is, the tendency for a subject to develop sign-tracking responses predicts that subject's vulnerability to drug addiction. This finding raises the intriguing possibility that sign-tracking may address a long-standing and fundamental question facing addiction scientists, "What are the pre-existing traits that make an individual particularly susceptible to becoming a drug addict?"

The Sign-Tracker Phenotype:

Some subjects respond to repeated lever-food pairings by approaching and contacting the lever. These subjects, called Sign-Trackers (ST rats), learn that the lever signals the impending delivery of the food, and they express this learning in an emotional way, revealing their attraction to the lever and their need to be in close proximity to it. This is the case even though approaching the lever serves no purpose and moves them to a location away from the site of the delivery of the food. Those subjects prone to exhibit sign-tracking responses also tend to exhibit a constellation of other addiction-related behaviors. ST rats tend to be more impulsive (Monterosso & Ainslie, 1999), quicker to respond, and to initiate action without due consideration of the longer-term consequences (Lovic, et al., 2011; Tomie, et al., 1998), contributing to their tendency to make riskier decisions (Olshavsky, et al., 2014). ST rats also tend to respond to novelty with arousal and excitement, rather than with caution (Beckmann, et al., 2011), which resembles sensation-seeking and thrill-seeking in addiction-prone animals (Piazza & Le Moal, 1996) and addiction-prone humans (Zuckerman, 1993, 2012).

Finally, and most significantly, sign-trackers are addiction prone. That is, ST rats develop drug self-administration responses more quickly (Beckmann, et al., 2011) and self-administer abused drugs more frequently (Saunders & Robinson, 2010). ST rats are more likely to experience cue-induced cravings for the drug's effects (Saunders & Robinson, 2013; Saunders, et al., 2013), and this increases the risk of relapse. ST rats are more vulnerable to cue-induced relapse, as assessed by post-extinction, cue-induced reinstatement of drug-taking (Saunders & Robinson, 2010). There is also evidence that ST rats, relative to GT rats, are more resistant to Pavlovian extinction procedures (Ahrens, et al., 2015). This suggests that Sign-Trackers will more likely maintain responding during cue-extinction therapy treatments, and, in addition, will more likely relapse into drug-taking when presented with a drug cue. ST rats also exhibit a constellation of physiological traits associated with vulnerability to drug abuse (Tomie, et al., 2000, 2004, 2008), as well as neurobiological markers differentially associated with elevated proneness to developing drug addiction (Flagel, et al., 2007). Therefore, addiction scientists have concluded that ST rats, subjects that tend to perform more sign-tracking responses, are also more likely to be addiction-prone (Flagel, et al., 2009). In this way, ST rats may represent the behavioral phenotype of the addictive personality (Jaffe, 1976; Kolb, 1962; Zilberman, et al., 2018; Zuckerman, 2012).

The Goal-Tracker Phenotype:

Addiction researchers have also noted that some of their subjects do not respond by approaching the lever that signals food. Rather, these subjects respond to the presentation of the lever by cautiously approaching the location of the food tray, where the food reward will soon be delivered. These subjects, called Goal-Trackers (GT rats), also learn that the lever signals the delivery of the food, but GT rats respond in a more cognitive and less emotional way, reacting to the information provided by the appearance of the lever that signals the imminent delivery of food. GT rats show little evidence of being attracted to the lever or having the need to be closer to it. Goal-Trackers, as compared to Sign-Trackers, tend to weigh the consequences of their actions more carefully, exhibiting less impulsive responding and more cautious behavior in risky situations. Current research has clearly shown that animal subjects of the GT phenotype are less addiction prone, relative to Sign-Trackers. Their introduction to drug use is a more gradual process. They are less likely to self-administer high doses of the drug, and less likely to relapse back into drug abuse.

Put another way, GT rats are reward-centric, while ST rats are signal-centric. Relative to ST rats, the behavior of GT rats indicates that they are guided primarily by their focus on the reward itself, while the behavior of ST rats, on the other hand, is controlled by and focused on, not so much the reward itself, but rather on the signal that predicts the reward. It seems ironic that GT rats, even though they are more focused on the reward, are less prone to addiction, while ST rats, even though they are less focused on the reward, are more vulnerable to becoming addicted (for review, see Meyer, et al., 2012).

It has been noted that ST rats react emotionally to reward-related cues. This is revealed by their pattern of reward cue-elicited actions, which include navigating to approach the location of the reward cue and then performing vigorous reward cue-directed consummatory actions. It has been suggested that sign-tracking may be the pre-existing marker or innate behavioral trait that confers vulnerability to drug addiction, or, in other words, the overt behavioral manifestation of the addictive personality (Flagel, et al., 2009; Saunders & Robinson, 2013).

Incentive Sensitization Theory:

The tendency to perform sign-tracking responses is a pre-existing behavioral trait that confers vulnerability to subsequently becoming addicted, but why is this so? What is the basis for the addiction vulnerability of the ST rat? According to Incentive Sensitization Theory (IST) proposed by Robinson and Berridge (1993, 2000), the cue-elicited emotional reactions of "craving" or "wanting" the drug are enhanced or sensitized due to repeated activations by abused drugs of the dopamine reward pathways (Meyer, et al., 2012). Consequently, drug cues increasingly trigger the feelings of "craving" or "wanting", which are responsible for the dramatically exaggerated motivation for drugs displayed by addicts.

Sign-tracking reveals, in the form of overt physical skeletal action, the sensitization of the incentive value or attractiveness of drug-related cues (Bindra, 1974). The emotions and subjective feelings of drug craving, drug wanting, and drug needing are aroused by the presence of drug-related cues and revealed by the physical expression of postural orientation and skeletal action of the target-directed behaviors of the freely moving ST rats. Thus, the propensity to attribute incentive salience to reward cues, to be attracted to reward cues, to approach reward cues automatically and reflexively, renders ST rats susceptible to drug addiction.

Humans have also been classified as Sign-Trackers or Goal-Trackers based on eye movements and gaze durations. For example, Garofalo and Di Pellegrino (2015) classified human subjects as Sign-Trackers if they directed eye-gazes toward the location where the visual signal, or as Goal-Trackers if they directed eye-gazes toward the location where the reward would be presented. When tested for voluntary reward-seeking behavior, Sign-Trackers exhibited stronger cue-triggered reward seeking than Goal-Trackers. Other investigators analyzed brain activity recorded using an electroencephalograph in response to food-related cues in obese and lean humans. They discovered two distinct cue-reactivity profiles. Sign-Trackers showed greater response to food-related cues but lower response to non-food pleasant stimuli compared with Goal-Trackers. More obese than lean subjects were Sign-Trackers and obese Sign-Trackers reported higher levels of emotional eating and food craving (Versace, et al., 2015). The notion that sign-tracking may be a pre-existing behavioral trait is supported by the finding that young children may be differentiated as Sign-Trackers or as Goal-Trackers (Joyner, et al., 2018).

How does sign-tracking relate to DA activity in the NAC (Parkinson, et al., 2002) and related pathways involved in the neurobiology of reward and addiction (Kuhn, et al., 2018; Robinson, et al., 2018)? The neurobiological pathways that differentiate ST rats from GT rats have been extensively studied, and while it is far beyond the scope of this book to detail the neurobiological brain substrates of sign-tracking, it should be noted that investigators have mapped the distinctive neurobiological substrates and have found that ST rats show stronger activation of DA in the NAC than GT rats (Kuhn, et al., 2018), and, in addition, ST rats also exhibit weak cholinergically-mediated cognitive/attentional control of the prefrontal cortex (Robinson, et al., 2018).

The ST and GT phenotypes model individual differences in vulnerability to substance use disorder. Investigators have noted in other paradigms additional examples of behaviors that are differentially associated with sign-tracking and goal-tracking. Symptoms of ST-like and GT-like responding are also observed in several other neuropsychiatric disorders. Based on the strong relationship between addiction and other psychiatric disorders, it is not surprising that sign-tracking has relevance to a broad range of neuropsychiatric disorders beyond just substance use disorders. Morrow (2018) notes overlapping behavioral symptoms and neuropsychiatric diagnostic criteria of ST-like effects observed in co-occurring neuropsychiatric disorders, including behavioral addictions, such as pathological gambling (Anselme, 2018; Robinson & Anselme, 2019), anxiety disorders, post-traumatic stress disorder (PTSD), psychotic disorders, and obsessive-compulsive disorder (OCD), while, GT-like symptoms are more prominent in individuals diagnosed with eating disorders, such as anorexia and bulimia, and depressive disorders.

Chapter 17: The Addiction Blind Spot

No one starts out using drugs with the intention of becoming a drug addict. And yet it happens. And each time it happens, the addict is largely, if not wholly, to blame. They took the drug. They took the drug repeatedly. No one forced them to do it. They did this to themselves. And yet, as noted previously, in the way we speak about addiction, we tend to make excuses for the addict, as though the addict played no role, beyond stumbling blindly into addiction, without knowing what they were doing. Our choice of words, when we speak about addiction, reveals that, in a very fundamental and prescient way, we recognize that addiction is not so much something that we do, as much as it is something that happens to us. Addiction is stealthy. And, this is because, as we are in the process of stumbling and falling into addiction, we are largely unaware of the changes that are taking place. Addiction creeps on us, and as it closes in, addiction is camouflaged by the illusion that quitting drugs is just a matter of deciding to stop.

In this chapter, we address the issue of the addiction blind spot (Tomie, et al., 2018). The complaints of the confused drug addict are telling. "I was blindsided," "I never saw it coming," "How did this happen to me?" Their words convey that they feel confused and cheated because they were unaware that their drug-taking would become unstoppable, persisting even when they were trying very hard to quit. Many addicts feel that they plummeted into the pit of addiction without fair warning, without any idea of the horrible dimensions of the awful consequences that awaited them. It was so unfair because they were not aware that their control of their drug-taking was slipping away, and they had no intention of ending up trapped like this.

On the road to becoming addicted, the user experiences the gradual erosion of self-control as their drug-taking takes on a life of its own, becoming increasingly automatic and reflexive. We propose that the underlying cause of it is the development of sign-tracking of drug-taking, and most significantly, the reason that sign-tracking of drug-taking goes unnoticed is because the reflexive use of drugs closely resembles and passes for voluntary drug-taking. This is the confusion created by the problem of mistaken identity. The naïve user is oblivious to the emergence of sign-tracking of drug-taking, which integrates seamlessly with ongoing voluntary drug use. This is the addiction blind spot, where drug-taking is gradually slipping out of control and the user is unable to see it. The drug addict is in the dark, unaware that sign-tracking is developing and is gradually robbing them of their free-will. The addiction blind spot is hidden by their lack of awareness that their actions have become triggered and reflexive due to sign-tracking. They remain confident in their ability to control their drug use, even as they lose their grip.

While treatment specialists have previously referred to an addiction blind spot, their focus was exclusively on relapse, that is, the pervasive tendency of recovering addicts to fall back into drug-taking (Formica, 2012; Reich, 2017). In their view, the blind spot that led recovering addicts to relapse was their ego-hypertrophic overconfidence, their tendency to discount their vulnerability to risk-taking. In contrast, the sign-tracking blind spot comes into play during a much earlier phase of the drug addiction process, when the user is just starting to get comfortable, settling into a routine, developing the habit of deciding to use the drug again and again. These repetitive acts of drug-taking tend to become ritualized, encouraging the development of sign-tracking, which is a form of drug-taking that the user is unable to control and the user will not be able to detect .. that the user will not differentiate from voluntary drug-taking.

Why is the user unable to see sign-tracking? The user is blind to sign-tracking because sign-tracking of drug-taking is camouflaged to pass for a voluntary act of drug-taking. Both responses look very much the same. They both consist of approaching, then contacting the object, then consuming the drug that is located inside the object. Not only do the two response forms closely resemble each other, they are also directed at the same target. Their target is the implement employed to consume the drug. It should come as no surprise, therefore, that when it comes to developing an understanding of what just happened, the user is faced with very limited set of readily available possibilities. The user is only aware of voluntary drug-taking, which constitutes, up to this point, the entirety of the user's drug-taking history. The user is boxed-in by his limited set of alternative explanations for the most recent act of drug-taking that was unintended and now requires processing. The user can only continue to interpret and process what just happened as just another act of voluntary drug-taking.

Cognitive Momentum:

Cognitive psychologists call this effect representational or cognitive momentum (Hubbard, 2015; Miura, 1990). That is, sign-tracking is especially likely to go undetected because of our tendency to see what we expect to see, and to see it as that which we have seen all along. The user has already established a history of performing voluntary acts of intended drug-taking; therefore, when sign-tracking performance of drug-taking does emerge, the user will misconstrue it as just another ordinary everyday routine act of voluntary and intended drug-taking. In other words, sign-tracking is simply overlooked because it is camouflaged to pass for what the user has come to expect to see, voluntary drug use. For this reason, sign-tracking is virtually invisible, allowing sign-tracking of drug-taking to hide in plain sight.

Thus, part of the problem, according to cognitive psychologists, is our tendency to see things as they were before. Early in the process, when drug use was initiated, drug-taking was strictly voluntary and intended, so that these repetitions of voluntary acts of drug-taking provided us with a presented pattern. Factors related to representational momentum and cognitive momentum favor forward projected displacements that continue this presented pattern (Freyd, 1987; Hubbard, 2010, 2015, 2017; Miura, 1990). With respect to drug-taking, the presented pattern is established by the repetitions of voluntary acts of drug-taking, so that additional instances of drug-taking are likely seen as the mere continuation of this previously established pattern. Due to cognitive momentum, the user is biased to see drug-taking as voluntary and intended, regardless of whether the drug-taking was a voluntary response or a sign-tracking response. The previously well-established presented pattern of voluntary and intended drug-taking influences the user who is observing sign-tracking, to mistake sign-tracking for just another voluntary drug-taking response.

Psychological Scotoma:

A visual scotoma is a blind spot in the visual field, due to a floater, a cataract, or other physical obstruction in the eye. A mental or psychological scotoma is a blind spot in our perception, in the way we view reality. It is, therefore, in a sense, a denial of reality. The denial of reality is a losing proposition that pits our perception against what is true. This is a battle that we can never win. In any dispute with reality, we must lose eventually (Paul, 2017). Such is the case with drug addiction, where turning a blind eye toward the loss of self-control can only make matters worse.

An analysis based on sign-tracking suggests that there is an addiction blind spot in the form of a psychological scotoma, which enables the gradual erosion of self-control to proceed unrecognized. Due to this blind spot the loss of self-control occurs in the background, at a preconscious level, without awareness. The addiction blind spot obscures the loss of self-control that fuels the transition from social, recreational, and voluntary drug use into the realm of the habitual and automatic drug-taking of the drug abuser. The question remains, why is the addiction blind spot so widely prevalent? Why are we unable to realize that we are losing control of our drug-taking?

An obvious way to account for the blind spot is to champion the possibility that this is merely a case of self-deception. Paul Simon noted in the lyrics of "The Boxer", "… but a man hears what he wants to hear and disregards the rest." (Simon & Garfunkel, 1970). There may be a measure of self-deception involved when drug addicts claim to believe that they were in control, even when they were not. Nevertheless, there may be many other factors, beyond mere self-deception, that lend assistance here, encouraging the addicts to believe that their drug-taking is voluntary.

Still another possibility to consider is neophobia, fear of the new or unfamiliar. Perhaps, it is in our nature to be fearful of new ideas. According to immunologist P. D. Medawar, the "The human mind treats a new idea the way the body treats a strange protein, it rejects it." (Medawar, 1986). The tendency to avoid accepting new ideas, to hang onto our favored and established point of view, may also contribute to the addiction blind spot. Beyond self-deception and neophobia, scientists have pointed to still other additional factors that may add-on to further cement the door and close the mind to the possibility of involuntary drug-taking.

A psychological scotoma is a mental activity in which one locks on to one idea and excludes all others. A psychological scotoma is a type of cognitive bias or confirmation bias, which is the tendency to search for, interpret, favor, and recall information in a way that confirms or strengthens one's prior point of view. According to political science Professor Brendan Nyhan people readily accept information that affirms their prior beliefs and are more critical of information that contradicts them. What we already believe to be true influences how we process information, making us more likely to think information we get is true if it confirms our predispositions and less likely to think it's true if it contradicts our preconceptions (Nyhan, et al., 2019). For example, the idea that I am in control of my drug-taking is locked in, while all other possibilities are locked out. In this way, I protect what I wish to maintain as my truth, even if it is not true.

Another part of the problem is the "illusion of control", our inclination to overestimate our ability to exercise control over events in our lives (Chapin & Coleman, 2009; Gouveia & Clark, 2001). The illusion of control is consistent with a pervasive optimistic bias that fuels the ego-hypertrophic overconfidence that causes the user to fail to internalize risk (Kendler, et al., 2003; Leyton & Stewart, 2014). The overconfident user believes that the risk of losing control of drug-taking is something that may happen to others, but it will never happen to them. They are in denial of how much they are at risk. The illusion of control biases the user to see themselves as always in control of their drug-taking, and this is the case even when there is evidence of self-control failure. For example, in studies with high-risk youth, the large majority of potential participants do not see themselves as having a problem, or even as being at risk for developing a problem, even though their scores on standardized questionnaires indicate otherwise (Wiers, et al., 2007).

WYSIATI:

To explain this egotistical overconfidence, Kahneman (2011) has introduced a concept that he labels What You See Is All There Is (WYSIATI). According to this theory of how the mind works, when the mind draws a conclusion, it deals primarily with what it knows. These are the phenomena that the mind has already observed, that is,

Known Knowns. In the case of addiction, the Known Knowns are the previously performed acts of drug-taking, which were uniformly voluntary and intended. Thus, the mind concludes that acts of drug-taking are voluntary and intended actions. In other words, because all my past acts of drug-taking were intended, then intended drug-taking is all that there is. According to Kahneman, the mind rarely considers Known Unknowns, phenomena that it knows to be relevant but about which it has no information. An example of Known Unknowns is where the mind has been warned of triggers, or has heard of addiction, but lacks understanding of how they work. Finally, the mind is completely oblivious to the possibility of Unknown Unknowns, which are unknown phenomena of unknown relevance, such as sign-tracking.

Thus, early on, according to WYSIATI, the pattern of voluntary and intended drug-taking establishes the Known Knowns as the full and complete set of all possible exemplars of drug-taking forms. It follows, therefore, that all acts of drug-taking that you may witness going forward will all be seen of this sort, that is, intended and voluntary. This is so because, with respect to drug-taking, intended and voluntary drug-taking acts are perceived as all there is. Because the mind of the user is unaware of the existence of sign-tracking, unaware of the possibility of involuntary and reflexive acts of drug-taking, the user is left to conclude that all acts of drug-taking must be voluntary.

Einstellung Effect:

Another factor that may contribute to the addiction blind spot is the Einstellung effect (Luchins, 1942). Einstellung is a German word that translates to setting, mindset, or attitude. The Einstellung effect is observed when the brain is stuck in a mind-lock or mindset, applying a previously successful approach to address a seemingly similar problem, even though the new problem is better addressed using a different approach. The Einstellung effect, therefore, is the negative effect of our successful previous experiences when solving new problems. The Einstellung effect occurs when a person is presented with a problem or situation that resembles problems that they have worked through in the past. If the solution to the problem has been the same in each of these past experiences, then the person will likely provide that same response, without giving the problem too much thought, even though a more appropriate response might be available.

In the case of drug-taking, the problem for the user is to account for why he took the drug. Early on, when drug-taking was being initiated, the user noted the intense euphoric effects of the drug. The problem for the user is to explain his drug-taking, and the solution, early-on, is that drug-taking is voluntarily performed to obtain the pleasurable effects of the drug. This account of his drug-taking is then applied to each of his subsequent acts of drug-taking. The Einstellung effect is observed when the user attempts to account for the newly emergent involuntary act of drug-taking. The user's solution to this seemingly similar but quite different problem is to quickly pass it off as simply another voluntary and intended action, performed to obtain the pleasurable effects of the drug. The user is mind-locked into recruiting a formerly appropriate solution, to a seemingly similar situation, when, in fact, a different solution is required.

Contingency Awareness:

Another factor that may contribute to the blind spot is the user's limited sense of awareness of the emerging positive contingencies between drug cues and the drug reward. These developing contingencies are by-products of habitual drug-taking, but they may remain in the background, unrecognized as drug cues. Their detection may be blurred by the complex and noisy texture of the stimulus background encountered during everyday living. The user may perform Pavlovian conditioned responses, including emotional or attentional sign-tracking-like behaviors, while, at the same time, remaining unaware of the triggers that elicit these reflexive responses.

Consistent with this hypothesis, there is experimental evidence that drug-associated cues may automatically trigger Pavlovian reflexive responses, even though the subject has no awareness that the cue has become associated with the drug (Leganes-Fonteneau, et al., 2018, 2019; Wiers, et al., 2007). For example, alcohol-related stimuli presented outside conscious awareness induced reliable changes in alcoholics' heart rates, and this effect was particularly pronounced in those alcoholics who scored high on craving for alcohol (Ingjaldsson, et al., 2003). That is, people may be unaware of the influence of drug-related cues on their drug-taking behaviors (De Houwer, et al., 2004; Krank & Swift, 1994). Functional MRI (fMRI) studies using subliminal (brief presentation of stimuli that are attended to but not consciously perceived) revealed that in cocaine abusers (Childress, et al., 2008) and marijuana abusers (Wetherill, et al., 2014) subliminal cues activate addiction-related brain areas without being consciously perceived. These data suggest that it is possible that the brain's response to reward cues may begin outside conscious awareness (Berridge & Winkielman, 2003), and this may contribute to the blind spot, to the inability of the drug abuser to identify triggers and process the emergence of reflexive drug-taking acts.

The addiction blind spot, the psychological scotoma, that leads the user to be unable to recognize that they are losing control of their drug-taking, is likely to develop because many of the predisposing factors that favor the development of the scotoma are present. For example: 1. Representational and cognitive momentum favor forward projected displacements that continue the presented pattern of well-controlled drug-taking, and; 2. The illusion of control biases the ego-hypertrophic and overconfident user to overestimate their control of their drug-taking while failing to internalize the risk of losing self-control, and; 3. Because of What You See Is All There Is (WYSIATI) the user, early on, sees only voluntary and intended drug-taking, and therefore, concludes that, going forward, voluntary and intended drug-taking is all there is, and 4. The Einstellung effect causes the user to apply an old solution to a new problem, accounting for the involuntary act of drug-taking by passing it off as voluntary and intended action to obtain the pleasurable effects of the drug, and 5. The lack of contingency awareness obscures the triggers of reflexive drug-taking. These psychological factors relate to the processing and filtering of the mind's representations of reality. They do not act alone. They interact with the physical properties of the drug use environment (drug rewards) that produce voluntary drug-taking, so that voluntary and reflexive drug-taking responses resemble each other and are targeted at the same location. The addiction blind spot, therefore, is created by the confluence of several factors that work together to blur the acuity necessary to distinguish reflexive acts of drug-taking from those that are intended.

How does sign-tracking contribute to the blind spot? What does sign-tracking have to do with the misguided belief of the drug abuser that they remain in full control of their drug-taking? The crux of the matter is the erroneous presumption of the drug abuser, who is only aware of voluntary drug-taking, who therefore believes that quitting is simply a matter of deciding to stop. This turns out not to be the case when the drug abuser tries but is unable to quit. Baffled and confused, the drug abuser resolves, once and for all, to dig in, make a stand, and mount an all-out, fully-committed resistance, vowing never to allow the drug to overrun them and ruin their life, ever again. The sworn pledge to turn over a new leaf is highly commendable, and certainly the well-intended thing to do, but wanting to quit, trying to quit, making the effort to quit, are ineffective weapons in the fight against a triggered reflex (Tomie, et al., 2016; Tomie & Sharma, 2013).

Therapeutic Tools:

The blind spot increases the risk of addiction by concealing from the user the evidence that they are losing control of their drug-taking, while simultaneously, increasing further their continued use of the drug. The remedy is to develop new tools to boost the user's ability to better recognize sign-tracking of drug-taking, and to improve their understanding of how the loss of self-control of drug-taking contributes to the development of drug addiction. Put another way, the drug user needs to change the way they think about their drug-taking. When they stumble, when they start to take drugs automatically, they must entertain a wider range of possible alternative explanations, beyond the usual "bad decision on my part". They must consider the possibility, disturbing as it is, that the act of drug-taking that they just performed was not intended. They must develop a better understanding of the origins of self-control failure. Only after seeing their behavior through that wider angle lens will the pertinent questions even occur to them. They must know enough to ask themselves, "Am I in control of my drug-taking?" "Was I triggered to have another?" "Am I sign-tracking?"

Learning about sign-tracking may change the way the drug user thinks about their drug-taking behavior. This is because sign-tracking can provide the user with novel perspectives and unique insights into features of drug addiction that have long remained mysterious and poorly understood (Tomie, et al., 2008). For example, consider the loss of self-control of drug-taking. While this is fundamental to drug addiction, it remains unclear why this happens. Sign-tracking provides an explanation that is based on empirical relationships among concrete events ... the loss of self-control of drug-taking develops due to pairings of the conduit with drug reward during repeated acts of voluntary drug-taking. This view creates a new focus for the drug user, charging them with the responsibility of monitoring the positive predictive relationship between the conduit and drug reward.

Consider another problem. Why is the drug abuser unable to see the loss of self-control of their drug-taking? While, as noted earlier in this chapter, numerous factors may contribute to the addiction blind spot, the sign-tracking analysis uniquely points to mistaken identity as the culprit, and, again, specifies the empirical relationships among concrete events that give rise to mistaken identity's masking effect. An analysis based on sign-tracking charges the drug user with the responsibility of periodically testing their control of their drug-taking, to ensure that the user can stop an ongoing drug-taking episode when stopping is intended. Developing a more comprehensive and more detailed understanding of sign-tracking and the relationships between sign-tracking and drug addiction will improve the adhesion of the observation of the act of involuntary drug-taking, so that the experience is less likely to be forgotten or discarded or overlooked. The objective is to equip the user with a more prominent cognitive conceptual peg to serve as an anchor, allowing the user to more effectively detect and retain evidence of loss of self-control of drug-taking.

Beyond the many ways that sign-tracking behaviors model prominent behavioral symptoms of drug addiction, there are also numerous similarities between sign-tracking and drug addiction in their physiological, neuroendocrinological, and neurobiological substrates (Everitt & Robbins, 2005; Robinson, et al., 2018; Tomie, et al., 2000, 2008). It is far beyond the scope of this book to detail the fascinating relationships between sign-tracking and the addicted brain, but we hope that this read will serve to whet the appetite and encourage further exploration.

Chapter 18: Educational Outreach

I f given the choice, I believe that a young person, who has never used any drugs, would choose to steer clear of becoming addicted. Not exactly a bold prediction, I fully realize, but there is a point to be made. Obviously, everyone would choose to avoid becoming a drug addict; yet, the sad truth is that addiction happens all the time. Apparently, merely knowing that addiction is to be avoided is not enough to steer you clear of it. As it now stands, naïve and uninformed individuals, particularly young people, initiate voluntary and social drug use without any understanding of the possibility that the act of drug-taking itself sets in motion the process of re-programming the brain to perform unintended and reflexive acts of drug-taking. To stem the epidemic of drug addiction, to stop the next wave before it starts, young people must be educated to become aware of sign-tracking before they initiate drug use.

Primary Prevention of Addiction:

The goal of primary prevention is to stop addiction before it starts … to help at-risk individuals avoid the development of addictive behavior. Primary prevention aims to prevent the initiation of drug abuse or delay the age of initiation of drug use, particularly among young people. Our primary prevention goal is to immunize against becoming addicted, to reduce the chances of becoming addicted before drug use has begun. Our goal is to introduce young people to the possibility of automatic, involuntary, reflexive drug-taking, which is a form of drug-taking that cannot be controlled. Our goal is for each of them to create in their head a mental file folder of sign-tracking, for future reference, so when they do perform an automatic act of drug-taking, they are not at a complete loss to understand it. Rather, because they have already formed the broader mental map, they are more likely to interpret and process that behavior as an instance of involuntary responding due to sign-tracking.

To introduce young people to sign-tracking, a creative writing team has been assembled, to use storytelling as a vehicle to communicate the idea of sign-tracking through a scientific short story. The team consists of Barbara Zito, storyteller and creative writer, Steven Petruccio, illustrator, and me, Arthur Tomie, addiction scientist. The scientific short story, *The Tail of the Raccoon: Secrets of Addiction* (Zito & Tomie, 2014, illustrated by Petruccio), was modeled on the scientific reports of the misbehaving raccoon (Breland & Breland, 1961, 1966). Students who knew nothing of sign-tracking were asked to read a short story about a raccoon who suffered the loss of self-control due to experience with object-reward pairings. Reading the story raised awareness in 9th-12th grade students of sign-tracking and the detrimental effects of losing self-control, relative to a control group that read a different short story (Levitch, et al., 2018).

This study provides evidence that young people who were previously unaware of the existence of sign-tracking can absorb the science lesson in the story, boosting their awareness of the existence of alternatives to voluntary action. The data reveals that it is possible to arm young people with knowledge of sign-tracking, and this serves to boost their awareness of the difference between voluntary action as opposed to involuntary and reflexive action. In this way, the young people may be armed with an improved mental map that includes a file folder of sign-tracking of involuntary action. This information may allow them to more quickly recognize the early indications that freedom of choice is slipping away and is being replaced by an automatic and reflexive form of behaving. To further the primary prevention objectives, we have also developed a short video, illustrated by Jayson Gotera, and narrated by Ruth Sulitzer. This YouTube video, entitled "The Tail of the Raccoon Book Trailer" is directed at parents of young children, encouraging them to read the scientific short story to their children, as a way of opening that conversation about drugs:

(https://www.youtube.com/watch?v=mWBb-zo_1yA).

Secondary Prevention of Addiction:

Secondary prevention programs target those individuals who have already started using drugs, with the aim of controlling the degree of damage to the individual by preventing drug use from developing further, to prevent drug-taking from becoming a more serious problem. Secondary prevention consists of uncovering or identifying potentially harmful drug use practices prior to the onset of overt symptoms of drug abuse or problems associated with abusing drugs.

If given the choice, I believe that a young person, who has already initiated voluntary use of their drug of choice, would choose to steer clear of becoming addicted. The life of the drug addict is not their goal, but social, recreational, voluntary, controlled and intended drug use is something they enjoy and not something they are eager or willing to give up. This is a bit of a dilemma. You do not want to give up your voluntary drug use, but, at the same time, you want to maintain control of your drug-taking, and you certainly want to avoid becoming addicted.

Our secondary prevention goal is to immunize the casual drug user against losing control of their drug-taking … to reduce their chances of stumbling and then falling into addiction. Our goal is to warn the casual drug user of the possibility of developing automatic, involuntary, reflexive drug-taking, that develops due to repetitions of voluntary acts of drug-taking. Our goal is to introduce the casual drug user to sign-tracking, so that they may create a mental file folder of sign-tracking, so when they do automatically perform an involuntary act of drug-taking, they are not at a complete loss to understand it. Rather, they have already formed the broader mental map that allows them to recognize that reflexive behavior as sign-tracking, rather than misconstrue the behavior as voluntary.

The creative writing team has developed a second illustrated scientific short story to use storytelling as a vehicle to communicate to the casual drug user the idea that sign-tracking of drug-taking may be induced by repeated acts of voluntary drug-taking. In the scientific short story, *The Tail of the Raccoon, Part II: Touching the Invisible, Illustrated* (Zito & Tomie, 2015, illustrated by Petruccio), the raccoon is induced to lose control of drug-taking due to repeated pairings of the silk vial conduit with the spider's intoxicating potion. Reading this scientific short story raised awareness, in the same 9th-12th grade students who read the first short story, of how drug-taking procedures lend themselves to the development of sign-tracking, and the subsequent loss of self-control of drug-taking, relative to a control group that read a different short story (Levitch, et al., 2018).

The two experiments reported by Levitch, et al., (2018), provide evidence indicating that young people who were previously unaware of the existence of sign-tracking can absorb the science lesson in the stories, thereby boosting awareness of the existence of an alternative to voluntary drug-taking. These studies reveal the possibility of arming young people with knowledge of sign-tracking through the reading of scientific short stories, and this serves to boost awareness of the distinction between voluntary drug-taking as compared to involuntary drug-taking. In this way, young people may develop a mental file folder labeled "sign-tracking" that provides the casual drug user with a broader range of possible explanations of drug-taking to consider. Thus, storytelling about sign-tracking significantly boosted awareness of the loss of self-control and improved understanding of how the loss of self-control contributes to the development of drug addiction

(Levitch, et al., 2018). Exposure to information about sign-tracking appears to allow young people to more quickly recognize the earliest indications that they are losing self-control of their drug-taking.

In addition, to further our secondary prevention objectives, we have developed an additional short video entitled "Blindsided by Addiction" (https://www.youtube.com/watch?v=gyhuEtpHANE). This video, edited and illustrated by Jayson Gotera and narrated by Victoria Tims and Daniel Tims, is directed at teens who are confused as they try to slow down their drug-taking, but continue to stumble, using drugs more and more. In the video, these teenagers are introduced to the first scientific short story, *The Tail of the Raccoon: Secrets of Addiction*, and as a result of reading the story, they see themselves behaving like the raccoon, triggered by reward-related cues and unable to stop themselves. They resolve to change their behavior by leaving the party earlier and removing themselves from the presence of the triggers that encourage the performance of automatic and involuntary drug-taking.

Tertiary Prevention of Addiction:

Tertiary prevention programs are sometimes referred to as addiction rehabilitation programs and relapse prevention programs. The aim of tertiary prevention programs is to minimize the problems that have developed due to prolonged drug use and to move the individual toward a drug-free life. The goal of tertiary prevention is to enable the individual to attain and maintain improved levels of functioning and health.

I believe that most drug addicts desperately wish they could quit, and if they somehow could manage to quit, I believe they would never ever intentionally do it again. They would never wish to repeat their same mistakes. Having experienced the horrors of addiction, they would be loath to recycle their misguided actions that got them addicted in the first place. And, faced with the opportunity for a do-over, their biggest fear would be getting re-addicted. They know that they do not want to return to the life of the drug addict, but apparently, that alone is not enough. The intention not to relapse is thick among addicts in recovery, but relapse rates remain highly elevated.

The Departures Thing:

The third video, entitled "Reflexive Drug-Taking, is illustrated by Jayson Gotera and narrated by Daniel Tims (https://www.youtube.com/results?search_query=reflexive+drug-taking). This video is directed at young people who are further along in their drug use, more involved with the drug scene. Jeff is regularly abusing alcohol and harder drugs while partying at the Rave club. Although warned by concerned friends about escalating drug use, Jeff seems unable to control his drug-taking, particularly while partying with his friends at the club. Finally, the club is rocked by a series of drug overdoses. A batch of tainted pills claims another overdose victim, a close friend, and then Jeff passes out while doing drugs at the club. Waking up in the emergency room is finally enough to shock Jeff into joining a therapy group. In recovery, Jeff builds a new circle of friends and by avoiding the Rave club and his former party buddies, Jeff manages to stay sober and clean.

The creative writing team has developed a third scientific short story to use storytelling as a vehicle to communicate to the drug abuser the idea that sign-tracking of drug-taking may trigger relapse to drug-taking. In the scientific short story, *The Tail of the Raccoon, Part III: Departures* (Zito & Tomie, 2016, illustrated by Petruccio), the raccoon is determined to quit the spider's intoxicating potion and live with his family along the shores of the lake, but he is not entirely free of memories of the potion's pleasurable effects. Yet, by removing himself from the vicinity of the spider's den and reminding himself of the depths of despair visited upon him by his obsession with the potion, the raccoon makes good on his promise to remain drug-free. Until, that is, he is tempted by the spider's confederate, who offers the raccoon a vial of the potion. Following several unsuccessful attempts at recovery, the raccoon and his family realize that he is a recurring triggered relapser, and he cannot live a drug-free life while remaining in his homeland. The young raccoon waves good-bye to his parents and siblings and notes the beauty of the Great Forest as he sets sail, alone, on a raft drifting slowly down the river, to build a new life, a drug-free life, away from any and all reminders of the potion's effects.

The lesson of the story is that addicts in recovery face a very tough choice. The addict must avoid the stimuli that are associated with drug use, the people, places, and things that were present while using. This is because when in the presence of drug-paired stimuli, the recovering addict will feel overwhelmed by cravings and urges that will trigger automatic, reflexive, involuntary, and unintended sign-tracking of drug-taking. That is, relapse to drug-taking is likely to be triggered by the mere presence of environmental stimuli that were present when the drug's rewarding effects were experienced. The addict in recovery is trying to quit and does not want to return to the misery of their life as a drug addict, but they set themselves up for failure, for relapsing back into drug use, when they allow themselves to be tempted, not realizing that temptation invokes a reflex over which they have no control. The addict must avoid all of the stimuli, all of the people, places, and things, that are mindful of the drug's effects.

The addict in recovery faces many challenges in building a drug-free life, including rejecting old party pals, and avoiding familiar hangouts, moving their residence, changing jobs, and dropping cell phone numbers and social media sites ... doing the departures thing. These are precisely the actions that must be taken to eliminate the sources of temptation that will blur your conscious awareness and activate the primitive reflexes of the ancient midbrain. Dozens of young people who have read *The Tail of the Raccoon, Part III: Departures*, some of them working in my research lab, others taking my lecture courses, still others attending meetings where I have given addiction prevention talks, have informed me that they were finally able to quit drugs but only after doing "the departures thing". In other words, they found that they were unable to abstain from drug use while remaining in their old familiar surroundings, among friends and co-workers and party pals, going to bars and taverns and clubs and concerts and ball games and barbecues and tailgates and back-yard parties and weddings and graduation celebrations, etc. As much as they truly wanted to quit, they simply could not resist when drugs were being used and the urge to join the party came upon them.

In one case, to remain abstinent, an individual found it necessary to re-locate far away, overseas, as far away as Egypt, where he managed to live a drug-free life. But, another individual, who also found it necessary to relocate overseas to sustain abstinence, discovered that staying away permanently was necessary. He found that after living overseas for over five years, he quickly relapsed when he came home to attend a family wedding. Thus, it appears that relocating to a faraway place is not a "geographical cure", but, rather is a treatment that suppresses cue-induced urges to use the drug. Several other students, I am told, did the departures thing when they moved from out of state or from North Jersey or South Jersey to New Brunswick, to enroll at Rutgers University. In moving their residence to attend college, they made sweeping changes to their employment situation and their place of residence. They came to college intending to build a new life, a more serious life, to start over with a clean slate, telling none of their former associates their new whereabouts.

Doing the departures thing, moving away and building a new life, is not easy, but the chances of sustaining a drug-free life are much better for those who leave than for those who stay. Those who attempt to quit drugs while remaining in their old familiar drug use environment, can expect to suffer cue-induced abstinence-induced withdrawal reactions and cue-induced cravings and urges to experience the drug's effects. Moreover, there is the ever-present temptation factor, where resistance is only as good as your weakest moment. For these reasons, the prognosis for recovery while remaining in the drug use environment is poor.

In giving talks to groups of young people, I am absolutely convinced that those who are initiating recreational drug use have never considered the possibility of becoming addicted and then having to do the departures thing. They have never even imagined the possible necessity of permanently relocating to escape addiction. In looking at their faces, it is clear they have heard of "people, places, and things" but they did not understand what it meant. It has never occurred to them that they may have to give up their family and their friends and everything that is familiar to them. They did not realize that using drugs in the presence of these people, places, and things, was making all of it toxic, contaminated, and unfit for living a drug-free life.

Cue-Induced Relapse:

The risk of relapse is great, and a big part of that risk is due to the lack of understanding on the part of the addict in recovery of the huge role played by the stimuli associated with drug use. Consider the role of the drug addiction context. The addiction context consists of the environmental stimuli that were present when the drugs were taken (Uslaner, et al., 2007). It is well-known that drug-taking is more rapidly reinstated when the recovering addict is in the drug-taking context (Tsiang & Janak, 2006). Rapid relapse to drug-taking may be provoked by the experience of abstinence, which is likely to be particularly unpleasant in the presence of stimuli associated with the use of the drug. Heroin addicts, for example, when abstinent and in the presence of the addiction context, report suffering intense dysphoria. Their bodies are wracked with intolerable pain. For heroin addicts treated in the United States and returned to their homes, relapse rates hover around 90%. Because of the presence of drug-paired contextual stimuli, heroin addicts in the United States typically suffer horrible withdrawal symptoms, and this contributes greatly to their tendency to relapse, again and again. The prognosis for most heroin addicts is dismal. Most are doomed to suffer decades of recurring relapses.

A remarkable and telling exception has been documented with United States military personnel serving in Vietnam (Spiegel, 2015). Based on drug-testing results, approximately 20% of U.S. servicemen in Vietnam were actively addicted to heroin. Upon returning to the United States, these servicemen were expected to require drug rehabilitation services, but the number of soldiers who continued their heroin addiction after they returned to the United States was shockingly low. Over 95% of the soldiers who were addicted in Vietnam did not become re-addicted when they returned to the United States. They reported virtually none of the typical symptoms of heroin withdrawal that have been extensively documented in those who became addicted to heroin in the United States. The obvious suggestion is that heroin addiction and symptoms of withdrawal are specific to the context in which the effects of heroin were experienced.

Several possible explanations of this context-dependent effect of heroin addiction have been proposed. One possibility is that the returning soldiers did not have access to heroin in the United States, limiting their relapse risk. But the soldiers reported few or any withdrawal symptoms, which is virtually unheard of in those addicted to heroin in the United States. Another possibility is that heroin addiction is misery-dependent (Hari, 2015). The soldiers were miserable in Vietnam, which led them to use heroin to self-mediate the intense pain of their unhappiness. Upon returning to the United States, the soldiers were no longer in a miserable state of intense suffering. They no longer felt the need to use heroin to self-mediate because their misery was specific to the horrors of combat in Vietnam.

Another possibility is that heroin addiction is stimulus bound … i.e., specific to the environmental stimuli that were present at the time that the effects of heroin were experienced. The soldiers experienced heroin's effects in the combat environment in Vietnam. They were with their combat buddies in the jungles of Vietnam. They were wearing camouflaged jungle fatigues, anti-flak jackets, and combat boots, while carrying weapons, ammunition belts, and other web gear. They were surrounded by the sights, smells, and sounds of war.

The military personnel in Vietnam typically smoked heroin while deployed "in the bush". Marijuana spiced with heroin was burned in the breech of a weapon, such as a M-79 grenade launcher or an M-60 machine gun, and then the smoke was drawn through the length of the barrel of the weapon, where the cooled vapors were inhaled. The weapon that was employed as a conduit to consume vaporized heroin was the single most positively predictive cue of the heroin high, but upon returning to civilian life in the United States, these weapons of war were not present. The wartime stimuli, including the people, places, and things that were associated with using heroin in Vietnam were simply not present in the United States. This suggests that the overwhelming desire to use heroin, that is typically observed during an abstinence or withdrawal episode, is due to the presence of environmental stimuli associated with heroin's effects, and in the absence of these heroin-related cues, the addict does not suffer the overwhelming urges to take the drug. Notably absent, upon returning to civilian life in the United States, are the weapons of war used to self-administer heroin in Vietnam.

Consistent with this stimulus-bound account of heroin addiction are the effects reported in the United States when convicted heroin addicts are released from prison and paroled back into the community. Upon being incarcerated, they had undergone mandatory heroin detoxification procedures, and had been repeatedly tested and medically cleared of all traces of heroin. After completing detoxification, and while serving the remaining months or years of their prison sentence, they suffered no heroin withdrawal symptoms. Nevertheless, upon being released from prison and paroled back into the jurisdiction of their drug use, they reported suffering intense cravings and overwhelming urges to use heroin. Notably, these cravings were triggered by the sight of cues in the neighborhood that were present when they used heroin. For example, the mere sight of the street corner where they had formerly conducted drug deals, triggered overwhelming cravings, urges, and desires for heroin's effects. Remarkably, these feelings were not present while they were in prison, where they had not experienced heroin use. The intense cravings compelled them to seek out and use heroin, even though they were fully aware that they were scheduled for mandatory periodic drug testing as a condition of their parole. According to the stimulus-bound account, the heroin addict will only experience the desire to use heroin when returned to the environment in which heroin use had previously occurred.

These data reveal that the cues associated with the drug's effects play a huge role in trapping the addict. These cues activate the processes underlying drug-taking, which are automatically engaged, resulting in the urge to engage in drug-taking that is very difficult to suppress. The cues associated with drug-taking become engrained with repetition and ritual, thereby contributing to continued drug use despite a conscious desire to abstain (Pierce & Vanderschuren, 2010). Drug-paired stimuli induce subjective cravings for the drug's effects (Cooney, et al., 1983; Fox, et al., 2007; Saunders, et al., 2013), as well as conditioned physiological responses (Carter & Tiffany, 1999). The persistence of these cue-elicited responses (Peters & De Vries, 2014) serve as nagging reminders of the drug's effects and drive the recovering addict toward relapse (Marlatt, 1990; Rohsenow, et al., 1994; Sinha & Li, 2007; Flagel, et al., 2016).

The Addiction Kindling Effect:

For an addict in recovery, the first attempt at abstinence is the most important. If the addict fails to maintain abstinence, if the addict relapses back into drug-taking, then the odds of recovery deteriorate and deteriorate even further with each subsequent failed attempt at recovery. This is the addiction kindling effect, which is a progressive disorder experienced by addicts after suffering multiple relapses. In simple terms, the kindling effect is the worsening of withdrawal symptoms with progressive relapses. Due to the kindling effect each relapse is followed by a marked increase in the likelihood and the severity of relapsing back into drug abuse (Becker, 1998; Reoux & Ries, 2001). In general, symptoms are more pronounced and longer lasting each time an addict fails to maintain abstinence and relapses back into drug use. With each relapse, the addict will return to drug use more quickly, use more heavily, and for longer binge periods.

The Stigma:

The recovering addict faces several challenges in achieving a drug-free life, including being stigmatized as a deviant, narcissistic, psychopath. The stigma is based largely on the conduct of the drug-sick drug-dependent addict whose overwhelming need to use the drug during episodes of abstinence-induced withdrawal lead to shameful and outrageous criminal behavior, including stealing from and assaulting family and friends. The stigma presents substantial obstacles to the recovering addict when attempting to acquire employment, housing, and social relationships. I am often asked if sign-tracking serves to frame the stigmatized misconduct of the addict in a more favorable light. Or, to put it another way, I am also asked if sign-tracking does not provide a convenient excuse for becoming addicted in the first place. After all, sign-tracking of drug-taking is not subject to control, and, sign-tracking of drug-taking is invisible. So, if you cannot control it and you cannot see it, how are your responsible for it? The point is that fighting sign-tracking, after the fact, is a losing proposition. Prevention of sign-tracking before it develops is the key to maintaining control of drug-taking, and our goal is to make it the responsibility of everyone to know about sign-tracking and to avoid developing sign-tracking. As described earlier, there are several protocols available to the drug user to discourage the development of sign-tracking, including diversifying drug-taking conduits, using specialized drug-taking implements to consume non-drug substances, and doing the departures thing. It is the responsibility of the drug user to avoid sign-tracking. This requires the user to regularly evaluate their control of their drug-taking, and to take effective measures to preserve their control of their drug-taking.

Conclusion: Implications of Sign-Tracking

The lesson here is that performing the action of consuming a drug may be involuntary. This behavior can occur automatically and without the involvement of conscious decision-making. Countless drug addicts have said to themselves, "I promised myself not to act that way, but I did it anyway." Drug rehabilitation clinics are filled with recovering addicts who are all too familiar with the feeling of being swept away because they reflexively and automatically reach out and take the drugs even though they are desperately trying to resist them.

This book is designed to bring about a better understanding of the phenomenon of sign-tracking and to illustrate how a casual drug user can slide so easily into drug addiction. Many drug addicts are filled with regret and want desperately to quit, but very few do so. The discovery of sign-tracking tells us why becoming addicted can be so easy while quitting can be so difficult. The message to young people is that drug use can be dangerous. The story is also intended to provide a better understanding of the problem of drug addiction for family and friends who simply cannot comprehend why their loved ones struggle so mightily to quit drugs, particularly when they are in an environment associated with drug use. The primary aim of this endeavor is to inform a younger audience of the scientific insights into the dangers of drug use and to add to the arsenal of tools available to those who are dedicated to drug education and prevention of drug abuse.

To build this awareness, we have developed educational materials (see Appendix A), including a series of scientific short stories, to convey via storytelling the scientific phenomenon of sign-tracking. Also, we have developed clusters of videos for parents and young people to introduce those who are in the midst of attempting to manage and control their drug taking to the scientific short stories, and finally, we have developed an educational website (www.tailoftheraccoon.com) to provide more detailed information for interested readers.

Our strategy is to introduce you to sign-tracking, as a way of opening your mind to the possibility of reflexive, involuntary, and unintended drug-taking. Our hope is that by reading this book and the educational materials in the Appendix, you can begin the process of breaking free of attributing all acts of drug-taking to pleasure-seeking, which we know is simply not true. Many acts of drug-taking are unintended, and just happen, out of habit, ritual, and reflex. You break out and move forward by creating an alternative category, a new mental file folder ...

a repository for collecting and processing acts of drug-taking due to sign-tracking. The goal is to reduce the risk of being blindsided, to avoid the stumble, to stay clear of falling into addiction.

Bibliography

Ahrens, A. M., Singer, B. F., Fitzpatrick, C. J., Morrow, J. D., and Robinson, T. E. (2015). Rats that sign-track are resistant to pavlovian but not instrumental extinction. *Behavioural Brain Research, 296*, 418-430.

Anselme, P. (2018). Gambling hijacks an ancestral motivational system shaped by natural selection. In J. Morrow & A. Tomie (Eds), *Sign-tracking and drug addiction* (pp. 106-128). Ann Arbor, MI: Maize Books.

Anselme, P., & Robinson, M. J. F. (2020). From sign-tracking to attentional bias: Implications for gambling and substance use disorders. *Progress in Neuro-Psychopharmacology & Biological Psychiatry, 99* ArtID 10986.

Anselme, P., Robinson, M. J., & Berridge, K. C. (2013). Reward uncertainty enhances incentive salience attribution as sign-tracking. *Behavioural Brain Research, 238*, 53–61.

Ballantyne, J.C., & LaForge, K.S. (2007). Opioid dependence and addiction during opioid treatment of chronic pain. *Pain. 129*, 235-255.

Balsam, P. D., & Gibbon, J. (1988). Formation of tone–US association does not interfere with the formation of context–US associations in pigeons. *Journal of Experimental Psychology: Animal Behavior Processes, 14*, 401-412.

Bates, M. E., & Labouvie, E. W. (1997). Adolescent risk factors and the prediction of persistent alcohol and drug use into adulthood. *Alcoholism: Clinical & Experimental Research, 21*, 944-950.

Beckmann, J. S., Marusich, J. A., Gipson, C. D., & Bardo, M. T. (2011). Novelty seeking, incentive salience and acquisition of cocaine self-administration in the rat. *Behavioural Brain Research, 216*, 159-165.

Bejerot, N. (1972). *Addiction: An artificially induced drive.* Oxford, England: Charles C. Thomas.

Berridge, K.C., & Winkielman, P. (2003). What is an unconscious emotion? (the case for unconscious "liking"). *Cognitive Emotion, 17*, 181-211.

Bindra, D. (1974). A motivational view of learning, performance, and behavior modification. *Psychological Review, 81*, 199–213.

Bitgood, S., Segrave, K., & Jenkins, H. (1976). Verbal feedback and the feature-positive effect in children. *Journal of Experimental Child Psychology, 21,* 249-255.

Blum, K., Sheridan, P. J., Wood, R. C., Braverman, E. R., Chen, T. J., Cull, G., & Comings, D. E (1996). The D2 dopamine receptor gene as a determinant of reward deficiency syndrome. *Journal of the Royal Society of Medicine, 89,* 396-400.

Brancato, A., Plescia, F., Lavanco, G., Cavallaro, A., & Cannizzaro, C. (2016). Continuous and intermittent alcohol free-choice from pre-gestational time to lactation: Focus on drinking trajectories and maternal behavior. *Frontiers in Behavioral Neuroscience, 10* ARTID 31.

Breland, K., & Breland, M. (1961). The misbehavior of organisms. *American Psychologist, 16,* 681–684.

Breland, K., & Breland, M. (1966). *Animal behavior.* New York: Macmillan.

Brevers, D., Cleeremans, A., Bechara, A., Laloyaux, C., Kornreich, D., Verbanck, P., Noel, X., (2011). Time course of attentional bias for gambling information in problem gambling. *Psychology of Addictive Behaviors, 25,* 675-682.

Brown, P. L., & Jenkins, H. M. (1968). Auto-shaping of the pigeon's keypeck. *Journal of the Experimental Analysis of Behavior, 11*, 1-8

Carnicella, S., Ron, D., & Barak, S. (2014). Intermittent ethanol access schedule in rats as a preclinical model of alcohol abuse. *Alcohol, 48* 243-252. Special Issue on Animal Models of Excessive Alcohol Consumption: Recent Advances and Future Challenges.

Carroll, M. E., & Lac, S. T. (1997). Acquisition of IV amphetamine and cocaine self-administration in rats as a function of dose. *Psychopharmacology (Berlin), 129*, 206–214.

Carroll, M. E., Morgan, A. D., Lynch, W. J., Campbell, U. C., & Dess, N. K. (2002). Intravenous cocaine and heroin self-administration in rats selectively bred for differential saccharin intake: phenotype and sex differences. *Psychopharmacology (Berlin), 161*, 304-313.

Carter, B. L., & Tiffany, S. T. (1999). Meta-analysis of cue-reactivity in addiction research. *Addiction, 94*, 327-340.

Case, A., & Deaton, A. (2020). *Deaths of despair and the future of capitalism*. Princeton, NJ: Princeton University Press.

Chapin, J., & Coleman, G. (2009). Optimistic bias: what you think, what you know, or whom you know? *North American Journal of Psychology, 11*, 121–132.

Cheatle, M. D. (2011). Depression, chronic pain, and suicide by overdose: on the edge. *Pain Medicine, 12*, S43-S48.

Childress, A. R., Ehrman, R. N., Wang, Z., Li, Y., Sciortino, N., Hakun, J., et al., (2008). Prelude to passion: limbic activation by "unseen" drug and sexual cues. *PLOS ONE, 3*:el 1506.

Cofresi, R. U., Bartholow, B. D., & Piasecki, T. M. (2019). Evidence for incentive salience sensitization as a pathway to alcohol use disorder. *Neuroscience & Biobehavioral Reviews, 107*, 897-926.

Congdon, P. (2019). Geographical patterns in drug-related mortality and suicide: investigating commonalities in English small areas. *International Journal of Environmental Research & Public Health, 16*, 1831.

Cooney, N. L., Baker, L. H., & Pomerleau, O. F. (1983). Cue exposure for relapse prevention in alcohol treatment. In R. J. McMahon, & K. D. Craig (Eds.), *Advances in Clinical Behavior Therapy* (pp. 194-210). New York: Brunner/Mazel.

Corbit, L. H., & Janak, P. H. (2016). Habitual alcohol seeking: Neural bases and possible relations to alcohol use disorders. *Alcoholism: Clinical & Experimental Research, 40*, 1380-1389.

Cottler, L., Phelps, D., & Compton III, W. M. (1995). Narrowing of the drinking repertoire criterion: should it have been dropped from ICD-10? *Journal of Studies of Alcohol, 56*, 173-176.

Crowell, C., & Bernhardt, T. (1979). The feature-positive effect and sign-tracking behavior during discrimination learning in the rat. *Animal Learning & Behavior, 7,* 313-317.

Cunningham, C. L., & Patel, P. (2007). Rapid induction of Pavlovian approach to an ethanol-paired visual cue in mice. *Psychopharmacology (Berlin), 192*, 231-241.

Dawe, S., Gullo, M. J., Loxton, N. J. (2004). Reward drive and rash impulsiveness as dimensions of impulsivity: implications for substance misuse. *Addictive Behaviors, 29*, 1389-1405.

Day, J. J., & Carelli, R. M. (2007). The nucleus accumbens and Pavlovian reward learning. *Neuroscientist, 13*, 148-159.

De Houwer, J., Crombez, G., Koster, E. H. W., & De Beul, N. (2004). Implicit alcohol-related cognitions in clinical samples of heavy drinkers. *Journal of Behavioral Therapy and Experimental Psychiatry, 35*, 275-286.

de Lint, J. (1973). *The epidemiology of alcoholism.* Toronto: Addiction Research Foundation of Ontario.

Delmar, M. (2015). I know that some of you don't understand. Foreword (pages ix-xi) in B. Zito & A. Tomie, *The tail of the raccoon: part III: Departures*. Princeton, NJ: ZT Enterprises LLC.

Destoop, M., Morrens, M., Coppens, V., & Dom, G. (2019). Addiction, anhedonia, and comorbid mood disorder. a narrative review. *Frontiers in Psychiatry, 10*, 311.

Diagnostic and statistical manual of mental disorders, fifth edition; DSM-5 American Psychiatric Association, Washington DC: APA Publishing,

Di Ciano, P., & Everitt, B. J. (2003). Differential control over drug-seeking behavior by drug-associated conditioned reinforcers and discriminative stimuli predictive of drug availability. *Behavioural Neuroscience, 117*, 952-960.

Di Ciano, P., & Everitt, B. J. (2004). Conditioned reinforcing properties of stimuli paired with self-administered cocaine, heroin or sucrose: implications for the persistence of addictive behaviour. *Neuropharmacology, 47*, 202-213.

Domjan, M., Lyons, R., North, N. C., & Bruell, J. (1986). Sexual Pavlovian conditioned approach behavior in male Japanese quail (*Coturnix cortunix japonica*). *Journal of Comparative Psychology, 100*, 413-421.

Everitt. B. J., & Robbins, T. W. (2005). Neural systems of reinforcement for drug addiction: from actions to habits to compulsion. *Nature Neuroscience, 8*, 1481-1489.

Falk, J. L. (1986). The formation and function of ritual behavior. In T. Thompson, & M. D. Zeiler, (Eds). *Analysis and integration of behavioral units* (pp. 335-355). Hillsdale, NJ: Erlbaum.

Falk, J. L. (1994). The discriminative stimulus and its reputation: role in the instigation of drug abuse. *Experimental & Clinical Psychopharmacology (Berlin), 2*, 43-52.

Falk, J. L., & Lau, C. E. (1993). Oral cocaine as a reinforcer: acquisition conditions and importance of stimulus control. *Behavioural Pharmacology, 4*, 597-609.

Falk, J. L., & Lau, C. E. (1995). Stimulus control of addictive behavior persistence in the presence and absence of a drug. *Pharmacology, Biochemistry & Behavior, 50*, 71-75.

Flagel, S. B., Akil, H., & Robinson, T. E. (2009). Individual differences in the attribution of incentive salience to reward-related cues: Implications for addiction. *Neuropharmacology, 56*, 139–148.

Flagel, S. B., Chaudhury, S., Waselus, M., Kelly, R., Sewani, S., Clinton, S. M., Thompson, R. C., Watson, S. J., & Akil, H. (2016).

Genetic background and epigenetic modifications in the core of the nucleus accumbens predict addiction-like behavior in a rat model. *Proceedings of the National Academy of Sciences, 113*, E2861-E2870.

Flagel, S. B., Robinson, T. E., Clark J. J., Clinton, S. M., Watson, S. J., Seeman, P., Phillips, P. E. M., & Akil, H. (2010). An animal model of genetic vulnerability to behavioral disinhibition and responsiveness to reward-related cues: implications for addiction. *Neuropsychopharmacology, 35*, 388-400.

Flagel, S. B., Watson, S. J., Robinson, T. E., & Akil, H. (2007). Individual differences in the propensity to approach signals vs goals promote different adaptation in the dopamine system of rats. *Psychopharmacology (Berlin), 191*, 599-607.

Formica, M. J. (September 15, 2017). Addiction's blind spot: Constancy, overconfidence, and conscious recovery. *Psychology Today*. Retrieved from https://www.psychologytoday.com/blog/enlightened./201205/addiction-s-blind-spot

Fox, H. C., Bergquist, K. L., Hong, K. I., & Sinha, R. (2007). Stress-induced and alcohol cue-induced craving in recently abstinent alcohol-dependent individuals. *Alcoholism: Clinical & Experimental Research, 31*, 395-403.

Freyd, J. (1987). Dynamic mental representations. Psychological Review, 94, 427-438.

Gallistel, C. R., & Gibbon, J. (2000). Time, rate, and conditioning. *Psychological Review, 107*, 289-344.

Gamzu, E., & Williams, D. R. (1973). Associative factors underlying the pigeon's key-pecking in autoshaping procedures. *Journal of the Experimental Analysis of Behavior, 19*, 225-232.

Garofalo, S., & di Pellegrino, G. (2015). Individual differences in the influence of task-irrelevant Pavlovian cues on human behavior. *Frontiers in Behavioral Neuroscience, 9*, 163.

Gouveia, S., & Clarke, V. (2001). Optimistic bias for negative and positive events. *Health Education, 101*, 228–234.

Gray, M. T. (2014). Habits, rituals, and addiction: an inquiry into substance abuse in older persons. *Nursing Philosophy, 15*, 138-151.

Grund, J. P. C. (1993). *Drug use as a social ritual: functionality, symbolism and determinants of self-regulation.* Rotterdam, Netherlands: Institut voor Verslavingsonderzoek.

Grunebaum, M. F., Hanga, C., Galfalv, Y., Oquendo, M. A., Burke, A. K., & Mannainsley, J. J. (2004). Melancholia and the probability of lethality of suicide attempts. *British Journal of Psychiatry, 184,* 534-535.

Hari, J. (2015). *Chasing the scream: the first and last days of the war on drugs.* London: Bloomsbury Publishing.

Hearst, E., & Jenkins, H. M. (1974). Sign-tracking: the stimulus-reinforcer relation and directed action. *Monograph of the Psychonomic Society.* Austin, TX: Psychonomic Society.

Heath, D. B. (1987). Anthropology and alcohol studies: current issues. *Annual Review of Anthropology, 16,* 99-120.

Heshmati, M., & Russo, S. J. (2015). Anhedonia and the brain reward circuitry in depression. *Current Behavioral Neuroscience Reports, 2,* 146-153.

Hubbard, T. (2010). Approaches to representational momentum: Theories and models. In R. Nijhawan, & B. Khruana, (Eds.), *Space and time in perception and action.* (pp. 338–365). Cambridge, UK: Cambridge University Press.

Hubbard, T. (2015). The varieties of momentum-like experience. *Psychological Bulletin, 141,* 1081-1119.

Hubbard, T. (2017). Toward a general theory of momentum-like effects. *Behavioural Processes, 141,* 50-66.

Hudson, A., Olatunji, B. O., Gough, K., Yi, S., & Stewart, S. H. (2016). Eye on the prize: High-risk gamblers show sustained selective attention to gambling cues. *Journal of Gambling Issues, 24*, 100-119.

Ingjaldsson, J. T., Thayer, J. F., & Laberg, J. C. (2003). Craving for alcohol and pre-attentive processing of alcohol stimuli. *International Journal of Psychophysiology, 49*, 29-39.

Jaffe, A. (1976). *Addiction reform in the progressive era: scientific and social responses to drug dependence in the United States 1970-1930.* New York: Arno Press.

Jellinek, E. (1960). *The disease concept of alcoholism.* New Haven, CN: College and University Press.

Jenkins, H. M., Barnes, R. A., & Barrera, F. J. (1981). Why autoshaping depends on trial spacing. In C. M. Locurto, H. S. Terrace, & J. Gibbon (Eds), *Autoshaping and conditioning theory* (pp. 255-284). New York: Academic Press.

Jentsch, J. D., & Taylor, J. R. (1999). Impulsivity resulting from frontostriatal dysfunction in drug abuse: implications for the control of behavior by reward-related stimuli. *Psychopharmacology (Berlin), 146*, 373-390.

Joyner, M. A., Hearhardt, A. N., & Flagel, S. B. (2018). A translational model to assess sign-tracking and goal-tracking behavior in children. *Neuropsychopharmacology, 43*, 228-229.

Kahneman, D. (2011). *Thinking, fast and slow.* London: Penguin Books.

Kelley, A. E., & Berridge, K. C. (2002). The neuroscience of natural rewards: relevance to addictive drugs. *Journal of Neuroscience, 22*, 3306-3311.

Kendler, K., Prescott, C., Myers, J., & Neale, M. (2003). The structure of genetic and environmental risk factors for common psychiatric and substance use disorders in men and women. *Archives of General Psychiatry, 60*, 929-937.

Kolb, L. C. (1962). *Drug addiction: a medical problem.* Springfield, IL: Charles C. Thomas.

Krank, M. D. (2003). Pavlovian conditioning with ethanol: sign-tracking (autoshaping), conditioned incentive, and ethanol self-administration. *Alcoholism: Clinical & Experimental Research, 27*, 1592-1598.

Krank, M. D., O'Neill, S., Squarey, K., & Jacob J. (2008). Goal- and sign-directed incentive: conditioned approach, seeking, and consumption established with unsweetened alcohol in rats. *Psychopharmacology (Berlin) 196*, 397-405.

Krank, M. D., & Swift, R. (1994). Unconscious influences of specific memories on alcohol outcome expectancies. *Alcoholism: Clinical & Experimental Research, 18*, 423.

Kuhn, B. N., Campus, P., & Flagel, S. B. (2018). The neurobiological mechanisms underlying sign-tracking behavior. In J. Morrow & A. Tomie (Eds), *Sign-tracking and drug addiction* (pp. 35-74). Ann Arbor, MI: Maize Books.

Kushner, M., Thurus, P., Sletten, S., Frye, B., Abrams, K., Adson, D., Demark, J. V. Maurer, E., & Donahue, C. (2008). Urge to gamble in a simulated gambling environment. *Journal of Gambling Studies, 24*, 219-227.

Labouvie, E., Bates, M. E., & Pandina, R. J. (1997). Age of first use: its reliability and predictive utility. *Journal of Studies of Alcohol, 58*, 638-643.

Leshner, A. I. (1997). Addiction is a brain disease, and it matters. *Science, 278*, 45-47.

Levin, J. (1990). *Alcoholism: a biopsychosocial approach*. New York: Hemisphere Publishing Corp.

Lewis, M. (May 2, 2019). The-sweet-spot-where-technology-meets-the-motivational-brain. www.nirandfar.com. Retrieved from https://www.nirandfar.com/ www.memoirsofanaddictedbrain.com

Leyton, M., & Stewart, S. (Eds). (2014). *Substance abuse in Canada: childhood and adolescent pathways to substance use disorders.* Ottawa, ON: Canadian Centre on Substance Abuse.

Locurto, C. M. (1981). Contributions of autoshaping to the partitioning of conditioned behavior. In C. M. Locurto, H. S. Terrace, & J. Gibbon, (Eds.), *Autoshaping and conditioning theory* (pp.101-135). New York: Academic Press.

Locurto, C. M., Terrace, H. S., & Gibbon, J. (Eds.). (1981). *Autoshaping and conditioning theory.* New York: Academic Press.

Loi, B., Lobina, C., Maccioni, P., Fantini, N., Carai, M., Gessa, G., & Colombo, G. (2010). Increase in alcohol intake, reduced flexibility of alcohol drinking, and evidence of signs of alcohol intoxication in sardinian alcohol-preferring rats exposed to intermittent access to 20% alcohol. *Alcoholism: Clinical & Experimental Research, 34,* 2147-2154.

Lovic, V., Saunders, B. T., Yager, L. M., & Robinson, T. E. (2011). Rats prone to attribute incentive salience to reward cues are also prone to impulsive action. *Behavioural Brain Research, 223,* 255-261.

Lubow, R. E., & Moore, A. U. (1959). Latent inhibition: The effect of non-reinforced preexposure to the conditioned stimulus. *Journal of Comparative & Physiological Psychology, 52*, 415-419.

Luchins, A. S. (1942). Mechanization in problem solving: The effect o Einstellung. *Psychological Monographs. 54*, 1–95.

Lynch, W. J., & Carroll, M. E. (1999). Sex differences in the acquisition of intravenously self-administered cocaine and heroin in rats. *Psychopharmacology (Berlin), 144*, 77-82.

Marlatt, G. A. (1990). Cue exposure and relapse prevention in the treatment of addictive behaviors. *Addictive Behavior, 15*, 395-399.

McCreary, D. R. (2002). Binge drinking in adulthood: the influence of gender, age, and beverage exclusivity. *International Journal of Men's Health, 1*, 233-245.

McCusker, C. G., & Gettings, B. (1997). Automaticity of cognitive biases in addictive behaviours: further evidence with gamblers. *British Journal of Clinical Psychology, 36*, 543-554.

McGrath, D. S., Meitner, A., & Sears, C. R. (2018). The specificity of attentional biases by type of gambling: an eye-tracking study. PLOS ONE 13, e0199990614-16.

Medawar, P. (1986). *Memoirs of a thinking radish: an autobiography.* Oxford, England: Oxford University Press.

Melendez, R. (2011). Intermittent (Every-Other-Day) drinking induces rapid escalation of ethanol intake and preference in adolescent and adult C57BL/6J mice. *Alcoholism: Clinical & Experimental Research, 35*, 652-658.

Meyer, P. J., Lovic, V., Saunders, B. T., Yager, L. M., Flagel, S. B., Morrow, J. D., Robinson, T. E. (2012). Quantifying individual variation in the propensity to attribute incentive salience to reward cues. PLOS ONE, 7,.0038987

Miura, T. (1990). Active function of eye movement and useful field of view in a realistic setting. In R. Groner, G. d'Ydewalle, & R. Parham, R. (Eds.), *From eye to mind: information acquisition in perception, search, and reading.* (pp. 119-127). North-Holland, England: Oxford Press.

Monti, P. M., Binkoff, J. A., Abrams, D. B. Zwick, W. R. Nirenberg, T. D. & Liepman, M. R. (1987). Reactivity of alcoholics and nonalcoholics to drinking cues. *Journal of Abnormal Psychology, 96*, 122-126.

Morrow, J. D. (2018). Relevance of sign-tracking to co-occurring psychiatric disorders. In J. Morrow & A. Tomie (Eds), *Sign-*

tracking and drug addiction (pp.162-185). Ann Arbor, MI: Maize Books.

Norton, G., Muldrew, D., & Strub, H. (1971). Feature-positive effect in children. *Psychonomic Science, 23,* 317-318.

Nyhan, B., Porter, E., Reifler, J., & Wood, T. J. (2019). Taking fact checks literally but not seriously? the effects of journalistic fact checking on factual beliefs and candidate favorability, *Political Behavior, 2019 (Jan).*

Olshavsky, M. E., Shumake, J., Rosenthal, A. A., Kaddour-Djebbar, A., Gonzalez-Lima, F., Setlow, B., & Lee, H. J. (2014). Impulsivity, risk-taking, and distractability in rats exhibiting robust conditioned orienting behaviors. *Journal of the Experimental Analysis of Behavior, 102,* 162-178.

Palfai, T. P. (2001). Individual differences in temptation and responses to alcohol cues. *Journal of Studies on Alcohol, 63,* 675-666.

Park, C. B., Park, S. M., Gwak, A. R., Sohn, B. K., Lee, J. Y., Jung, H. Y., Chow, S. W., Kim, D. J., & Choi, J. S. (2015). The effect of repeated exposure to virtual gambling cues on the urge to gamble. *Addictive Behavior, 41,* 64-64.

Parkinson, J. A., Dalley, J. W., Cardinal, R. N., Bamford, A., Fehnert, B., Lachenal, G., Rudarankanchana, N., Halkerston, K. M., Robbins, T. W., & Everitt, B. J. (2002). Nucleus accumbens dopamine depletion impairs both acquisition and performance of appetitive Pavlovian approach behaviour: implications for mescoaccumbens dopamine function. *Behavioural Brain Research, 137*, 149-163.

Paul, G. (November 30, 2017). How psychological scotoma keeps you trapped in addiction. www.hope-rehab-center-thailand.com. Retrieved from: https://www.hope-rehab-center-thailand.com › Posts ›Blog › Addiction, Personal Development.

Peris, J., Rhodes, N., McCullough, B., Aramini, R., & Zharikova, A. (2015). Intermittent high-dose ethanol exposure increases ethanol preference in rats. *Journal of Studies on Alcohol and Drugs, 76*, 165-173.

Peters J., & De Vries T. J. (2014). Pavlovian conditioned approach, extinction, and spontaneous recovery to an audiovisual cue paired with an intravenous heroin infusion. *Psychopharmacology (Berlin) 231*, 447–453.

Piazza, P. V., & Le Moal, M. (1996). Pathophysiological basis of vulnerability to drug abuse: role of an interaction between stress, glucocorticoids, and dopaminergic neurons. *Annual Review of Pharmacology & Toxicology, 36,* 359-378.

Pierce, R. C., & Vanderschuren, L. J. (2010). Kicking the habit: The neural basis of ingrained behaviors in cocaine addiction. *Neuroscience & Biobehavioral Reviews, 35,* 212-219.

Potenza, M. N., Steinberg, M. A., Skudlarski, P., Fulbright, R. K., Lacadie, C. M., Wilber, M. K., Rounsaville, B. J., Gore, J. C., & Wexler, B. E. (2003). Gambling urges in pathological gambling: a functional magnetic resonance imaging study. *Archives of General Psychiatry, 60,* 838-836.

Reich, C. (November 14, 2017). Understanding the Blind Spot in Addiction. www.therapyinsider.com. Retrieved from https://www.therapyinsider.com/FeedItem/Understanding-the-Blind-Spot-in-Addiction/

Robinson, T. E., Carr, C., & Kawa, A. B. (2018). The propensity to attribute incentive salience to drug cues and poor cognitive control combine to render Sign-Trackers susceptible to addiction. In J. Morrow, & A. Tomie (Eds), *Sign-tracking and drug addiction* (pp. 75-105). Ann Arbor, MI: Maize Books.

Robinson, T. E., & Berridge, K. C. (1993). The neural basis of drug craving: an incentive-sensitization theory of addiction. *Brain Research Reviews, 18*, 247-291.

Robinson, T. E., & Berridge, K. C. (2000). The psychology and neurobiology of addiction: an incentive-sensitization view. *Addiction, 95 Suppl 2*, S91-117.

Robinson, T. E., & Berridge, K. C. (2001). Incentive-sensitization and addiction. *Addiction. 96*, 103-114.

Rohsenow, D. J., Monti, P. M., Rubonis, A. V., Sirota, A. D., Niaura, R. S., Colby, S., Wunschel, S. M., & Abrahms, D. B. (1994). Cue reactivity as a predictor of drinking among male alcoholics. *Journal of Consulting & Clinical Psychology, 63*, 620-626.

Roth, M. E., Casimir, A. G., & Carroll, M. E. (2002). Influence of estrogen in the acquisition of intravenously self-administered heroin in female rats. *Pharmacology, Biochemistry & Behavior, 72*, 313-318.

Sabino, V., Kwak, J., Rice, K. C., & Cottone, P. (2013). Pharmacological characterization of the 20% alcohol intermittent access model in Sardinian alcohol-preferring rats: a model of binge-like drinking. *Alcoholism: Clinical & Experimental Research, 37*, 635-643.

Sainsbury, R. S. (1971). Effect of proximity of element on the feature-positive effect. *Journal of the Experimental Analysis of Behavior, 16*, 315-325.

Saunders, B. T., & Robinson, T. E. (2010). A cocaine cue acts as an incentive stimulus in some but not others: implications for addiction. *Biological Psychiatry, 67*, 730-736.

Saunders, B. T., & Robinson, T. E. (2013). Individual variation in resisting temptation: implications for addiction. *Neuroscience & Biobehavioral Reviews, 37*, 1955-1975.

Saunders, B. T., Yager, L. M., & Robinson, T. E. (2013). Cue-evoked cocaine "craving": role of dopamine in the accumbens core. *Journal of Neuroscience, 33*, 13989–14000.

Schwartz, B. (1975). Discriminative stimulus location as a determinant of positive and negative behavioral contrast in the pigeon. *Journal of the Experimental Analysis of Behavior, 23*, 167-176.

Schwartz, B., & Gamzu, E. (1977). Pavlovian control of operant behavior: An analysis of autoshaping and its implications for operant conditioning. In W. K. Honig, & J. E. R. Staddon (Eds.), *Handbook of operant behavior.* Englewood Cliffs, NJ: Prentice-Hall.

Schwartz, B., Hamilton, B., & Silberberg, A. (1975). Behavioral contrast in the pigeon: A study of the duration of key pecking maintained on multiple schedules of reinforcement. *Journal of the Experimental Analysis of Behavior, 24*, 199-206.

Schwartz, B., & Williams, D. (1972). Two different kinds of key peck in the pigeon: Some properties of responses maintained by negative and positive response-reinforcer contingencies. *Journal of the Experimental Analysis of Behavior, 18*, 201-216.

Sherman, M. E., Jorenby, M. S., & Baker, T. B. (1989). Classical conditioning with alcohol: Acquired preferences and aversions, tolerance, and urges/cravings. In D. A. Wilkinson, & D Chandron (Eds.), *Theories of alcoholism* (pp. 173-237). Toronto: Addiction Research Foundation.

Simms, J. A., Nielsen, C. K., Li, R., & Bartlett, S. E. (2013). Intermittent access ethanol consumption dysregulates CRF function in the hypothalamus and is attenuated by the CRF- R1 antagonist, CP-376395. *Addiction Biology, 19*, 606-611.

Simms, J. A., Steensland, P., Medina, B., Abernathy, K. E., Chandler, L. J., Wise, R., & Bartlett, S. E. (2008). Intermittent access to 20% ethanol induces high ethanol consumption in Long–Evans and Wistar rats. *Alcoholism: Clinical & Experimental Research, 32*, 1816-1823.

Simon, P. & Garfunkel, A. (February 2, 2019). "The Boxer" by Simon & Garfunkel, 1970, on the album, *Bridge Over Troubled Waters*. https://genius.com. Retrieved from https://genius.com/Simon-and-garfunkel-the-boxer-lyrics.

Sinha, R., & Li, C. (2007). Imaging stress- and cue-induced drug and alcohol craving: association with relapse and clinical implications. *Drug & Alcohol Reviews, 26,* 25-31.

Solomon, R. L., & Corbit, J. D. (1978). An opponent-process theory o. motivation. *The American Economic Review, 68,* 12-24.

Sparber, S. D., Bollweg, G. L., & Messing, R. B. (1991). Food deprivation enhances both autoshaping and autoshaping impairment by a latent inhibition procedure. *Behavioural Processes, 23,* 59-74.

Spiegel, A. (October 12, 2015). *What heroin addiction tells us about changing bad habits.* http://www.npr. Retrieved from http://www.npr.org/sections/health-shots/2015/01/05/371894919.

Spoelder, M., Flores Dourojeanni, J. P., de Git, K. C. G., Baars, A. M., Lesscher, H. M. B., & Vanderschuren, L. J. M, J. (2017). Individual differences in voluntary alcohol intake in rats: relationship with impulsivity, decision making and Pavlovian conditioned approach. *Psychopharmacology (Berlin), 234,* 2177-2196.

Stahl, J. (1995). *Permanent midnight. a memoir*. New York, NY: Warner Books.

Stewart, J., de Wit, H., & Eikelboom, R. (1984). The role of unconditioned and conditioned drug effects in the self-administration of opiates and stimulants. *Psychological Review, 91*, 251-268.

Stiers, M., & Silberberg, A. (1974). Lever-contact responses in rats: Automaintenance with and without a negative response-reinforcer dependency. *Journal of the Experimental Analysis of Behavior, 22*, 497-506.

Tiffany, S. T. (1990). A cognitive model of drug urges and drug-use behavior: Role of automatic and nonautomatic processes. *Psychological Review, 97*, 147-168.

Tomie, A. (1995). CAM: An animal learning model of excessive and compulsive implement-assisted drug-taking in humans. *Clinical Psychology Review, 15*, 145–167.

Tomie, A. (1996). Locating reward cue at response manipulandum (CAM) induces symptoms of drug abuse. *Neuroscience & Biobehavioral Reviews, 20*, 505–535.

Tomie, A. (2001). Autoshaping and drug-taking. In R. R. Mowrer, & S G. Klein (Eds). *Handbook of contemporary learning theories* (pp. 409-438). Mahwah, NJ: Erlbaum.

Tomie, A. (2018a). Autoshaping. In J. Vonk and T. K. Shackelford (Eds.), *Encyclopedia of animal cognition and behavior*, open acces: e-book, Springer.

Tomie, A. (2018b). Introduction: The role of sign-tracking in drug addiction. In J. Morrow and A. Tomie (Eds.), *Sign-tracking and drug addiction* (pp. 1-7). Ann Arbor, MI: Maize Books.

Tomie, A., Aguado, A. S., Pohorecky, L. A., & Benjamin, D. (2000). Individual differences in pavlovian autoshaping of lever pressing in rats predict stress-induced corticosterone release and mesolimbic levels of monoamines. *Pharmacology, Biochemistry & Behavior, 65*, 509-517.

Tomie, A., Badawy, N., & Rutyna, J. (2016). *Sign-tracking model of loss of self-control of drug-taking.* Berlin, Germany: Avid Science.

Tomie, A., Di Poce, J., Derenzo, C. C., & Pohorecky, L. A. (2002). Autoshaping of ethanol drinking: an animal model of binge drinking. *Alcohol & Alcoholism, 37*, 138-146.

Tomie, A., Grimes, K. L., & Pohorecky, L. A. (2008). Behavioral characteristics and neurobiological substrates shared by Pavlovian sign-tracking and drug abuse. *Brain Research Reviews, 58,* 121–135.

Tomie, A., Jeffers, P., & Zito, B. (2018). Sign-tracking model of the addiction blind spot. In J. Morrow, & A. Tomie (Eds), *Sign-tracking and drug addiction* (pp. 8-34), Ann Arbor, MI: Maize Books.

Tomie, A., & Sharma, N. (2013). Pavlovian sign-tracking model of alcohol abuse. *Current Drug Abuse Reviews, 6,* 201–219.

Tomie, A., Brooks, W., & Zito, B. (1989). Sign-tracking: the search for reward. In S. B. Klein, & R. R. Mowrer (Eds.), *Contemporary learning theories: Pavlovian conditioning and the status of traditional learning theory* (pp. 191-223). Hillsdale, NJ: Erlbaum.

Tomie, A., Cunha, C., Mosakowski, E. M., Quartarolo, N. M., Pohorecky, L. A., & Benjamin, D. (1998). Effects of ethanol on Pavlovian autoshaping in rats. *Psychopharmacology (Berlin), 139,* 154-159.

Tomie, A., Festa, E. D., Sparta, D. R., & Pohorecky, L. A. (2003a). Lever conditioned stimulus-directed autoshaping induced by saccharin-ethanol unconditioned stimulus solution: effects of ethanol concentration and trial spacing. *Alcohol, 30,* 35-44.

Tomie, A., Gittleman, J., Dranoff, E., & Pohorecky, L. A. (2005). Social interaction opportunity and intermittent presentations of ethanol sipper tube induce ethanol drinking in rats. *Alcohol, 35*, 43-55.

Tomie, A., Wong, K., Apor, K., Patterson-Buckendahl, P., & Pohorecky, L. A. (2003b). Autoshaping of ethanol drinking in rats: effects of ethanol concentration and trial spacing. *Alcohol, 31*, 125-135.

Tomie, A., Miller, W. C., Dranoff, E., & Pohorecky, L. A. (2006). Intermittent presentations of ethanol sipper tube induce ethanol drinking in rats. *Alcohol & Alcoholism, 41*, 219-225.

Tranberg, D. K., & Rilling, M. (1978). Latent inhibition in the autoshaping paradigm. *Bulletin of the Psychonomic Society, 11*, 273-276.

Tsiang, M. T., & Janak, P. H. (2006). Alcohol seeking in C57BL/6 mice induced by conditioned cues and contexts in the extinction-reinstatement model. *Alcohol, 38*, 84-88.

Tunstall, B. J., & Kearns, D. N. (2014). Sign-tracking predicts increased choice of cocaine over food in rats. *Behavioural Brain Research, 281*, 222-228.

Uslaner, J. M., Acerbo, M. J., Jones, S. A., & Robinson, T. E. (2006). The attribution of incentive salience to a stimulus that signals an intravenous injection of cocaine. *Behavioural Brain Research, 169,* 320-324.

Uslaner, J. M., Crombag, H. S., & Robinson, T. E. (2007). The influence of environmental context on the effects of drugs of abuse. In A. Kalechstein, & W. van Gorp, (Eds.), *Neuropsychology and substance use: state of the art and future directions* (pp. 435-456). Philadelphia, PA: Taylor & Francis.

Versace, F., Kypriotakis, G., Basen-Engquist, K., & Schembre, S. M. (2015). Heterogeneity in brain reactivity to pleasant and food cues: evidence of sign-tracking in humans. *Social, Cognitive & Affective Neuroscience, nsv143.*

Volkow, N. D., Koob, G. F. & McLellan, A. T. (2016). Neurobiologic advances from the brain disease model of addiction. *The New England Journal of Medicine, 374,* 363–371.

Volkow, N. D., & Morales, M. (2015). The brain on drugs: from reward to addiction. *Cell, 162,* 712-725.

Volkow, N. D., Wang, G. J., Fowler, J. S., Tomasi, D., & Telang, F. (2010). Addiction: Beyond dopamine reward circuitry. *Proceedings of the National Academy of Sciences of the United States of America, 108,* 15037-15042.

Volkow, N. D., Baler, R. D., & Goldstein, R. Z. (2011). Addiction: pulling at the neural threads of social behaviors. *Neuron, 69*, 599-601.

Wetherill, R. G., Childress, A. R., Jagannathan, K, Bender, J, Young, K. A., Suh, J. J., O'Brien, C. P., & Franklin, T. R. (2014). Neural response to subliminally presented cannabis and other emotionally evocative cues in cannabis-dependent individuals. *Psychopharmacology (Berlin), 231*, 2397-1407.

White, H. R., Labouvie, E. W., & Papadaratsakis, V. (2005). Changes in substance use during the transition to adulthood: a comparison of college students and their noncollege age peers. *Journal of Drug Issues, 35*, 281-306.

White W. L. (1996). *Pathways: from the culture of addiction to the culture of recovery. a travel guide for addiction professionals. 2nd ed.* Center City, MN: Hazelden.

Wiers, C. E., Zhao, J., Manza, P., Murani, K., Ramirez, V., Zehra, A., Freeman, C., Yuan, K., Wang, G., Demiral, S. B., Childress, A. R., Tomasi, D., & Volkow, N.D. (2020). Conscious and unconscious brain responses to food and cocaine cues. *Brain Imaging and Behavior.* Mar 3. doi: 10.1007/s11682-020-00258-x.

Wiers, R. W., Bartholow, B. D., van den Wildenberg, E., Thush, C., Engels, R. C. M. E., Sher, K. J., Grenard, J., Ames, S. L., & Stacy, A. W. (2007). Automatic and controlled processes and the development of addictive behaviors in adolescents: a review and a model. *Pharmacology, Biochemistry & Behavior, 86,* 263-283.

Williams, D. R., & Williams, H. (1969). Auto-maintenance in the pigeon: sustained pecking despite contingent non-reinforcement. *Journal of the Experimental Analysis of Behavior, 12,* 511–520.

Wilt, G. E., Lewis, B. E., Adams, E. E. (2019). A spatial exploration of changes in drug overdose mortality in the United States, 2000–2016. *Previews of Chronic Disease, 16,* 180405.

Wise, R. A. (2004). Dopamine, learning and motivation. *National Review of Neuroscience, 5,* 483-494.

Woolf, S. H., & Schoomaker, H. (1996). Life expectancy and mortality rates in the United States, 1959-2017. *Journal of the American Medical Association, 322,* 20.

Wulfert, E., Maxson, J., & Jardin, B. (2009). Cue-specific reactivity in experienced gamblers. *Psychology of Addictive Behaviors, 23,* 731-735.

Zilberman, N., Yadid, G., Efrati, Y., Neumark, Y. & Rassovsky, Y. (2018). Personality profiles of substance and behavioral addictions. *Addictive Behaviors, 82,* 174-181.

Zito, B., & Tomie, A. (2014). *The tail of the raccoon: Secrets of addiction.* Princeton, NJ: ZT Enterprises, LLC. Paperback, Createspace, 70 pages.

Zito, B., & Tomie, A. (2015). *The tail of the raccoon, part II: Touching the invisible.* Princeton, NJ: ZT Enterprises, LLC. Paperback, Createspace, 171 pages.

Zito, B., & Tomie, A. (2016). *The tail of the raccoon, part III: Departures.* Princeton, NJ: ZT Enterprises, LLC. Paperback, Createspace, 181 pages

Zuckerman, M. (1993). Sensation seeking and impulsivity: a marriage of traits made in biology? In McCown, W.G., Johnson, J.L., & Shure, M.B. (Eds.), *The impulsive client: theory, research, and treatment,* (pp. 71-91). Washington, DC: American Psychological Association.

Zuckerman, M. (2012). Psychological factors and addiction: personality. In H. Shaffer, D. A. LaPlante, & S. E. Nelson, (Eds.), *APA addiction syndrome handbook, vol. 1: foundations, influences and expressions of addiction*, (pp. 175-194). Washington DC: American Psychological Association.

Appendix A

Scientific Short Stories of

The Sign Tracker Trilogy:

Text-Only:

Zito, B., & Tomie, A. (2014). *The tail of the raccoon: secrets of addiction.* Princeton, NJ: ZT Enterprises, LLC. Paperback, Createspace, 70 pages.

Zito, B., & Tomie, A. (2015). *The tail of the raccoon, part II: touching the invisible.* Princeton, NJ: ZT Enterprises, LLC. Paperback, Createspace, 171 pages.

Zito, B., & Tomie, A. (2016). *The tail of the raccoon, part III: departures.* Princeton, NJ: ZT Enterprises, LLC. Paperback, Createspace, 181 pages.

Scientific Short Stories of

The Sign Tracker Trilogy:

Illustrated:

Zito, B., & Tomie, A. (2015). *The tail of the raccoon: secrets of addiction (illustrated)*. Princeton, NJ: ZT Enterprises, LLC. Paperback, Createspace, 63 pages.

Zito, B., & Tomie, A. (2019). *The tail of the raccoon, part II: touching the invisible (illustrated)*. Cranbury, NJ: ZT Enterprises, LLC. Paperback, Createspace, 104 pages.

Zito, B., & Tomie, A. (2019). *The tail of the raccoon, part III: departures (illustrated)*. Princeton, NJ: ZT Enterprises, LLC. Paperback, Createspace, 106 pages.

Scientific Short Stories of

The Sign Tracker Trilogy:

<u>E-Book:</u>

Zito, B., & Tomie, A. (2014). *The tail of the raccoon: secrets of addiction*. Princeton, NJ: ZT Enterprises, LLC. E-reader. Kindle Direct Publishing, 32 pages. Retrieved from https://www.amazon.com/dp/B00I3TNYJY

Zito, B., & Tomie, A. (2015). *The tail of the raccoon, part II: touching the invisible*. Princeton, NJ: ZT Enterprises, LLC. E-reader. Kindle Direct Publishing, 119 pages. Retrieved from http://www.amazon.com/Tail-Raccoon-Part-II-Invisible/dp/0991349555/ref=tmm_pap_swatch_0?_encoding=UTF 8&qid=&sr

Zito, B., & Tomie, A. (2016). *The tail of the raccoon, part III: departures*. E-reader. Kindle Direct Publishing, 119 pages. https://www.amazon.com/Tail-Raccoon-Part-III-Departures-ebook/dp/B01FZKDV6O/ref=sr_1_2?dchild=1&keywords=The

Educational Videos:

Title of Video: Who Doesn't Love a Good Story?,
https://youtu.be/Ik7UyShhqKs

Title of Video: The Tail of the Raccoon Book Trailer,

https://www.youtube.com/watch?v=mWBb-zo_1yA

Title of Video: Blindsided by Addiction,

https://www.youtube.com/watch?v=gyhuEtpHANE

Title of Video: Reflexive Drug-Taking,

https://www.youtube.com/watch?v=zTIGgWfY92U&t=64s

Title of Video: Raccoon Behavior Exhibiting Sign-Tracking,
https://www.youtube.com/watch?v=D52sQJEQI0Y

Title of Video: Sign-Tracking Lever Paired with Food,

https://www.youtube.com/watch?v=x38b0R6TZxM&t=7s

Glossary

Anhedonia: Noun; medicine, an inability to experience the emotional state of pleasure from activities usually found enjoyable.

Beguile: Verb; to charm or enchant (someone), sometimes in a deceptive way; to win over, woo, or captivate.

Catheter: Noun; medicine, a flexible tube inserted through a narrow opening into a body cavity, to deliver or remove fluid.

Cholinergic: Adjective; physiology, relating to or denoting nerve cells (neurons) in which a chemical, acetylcholine, produced by the neuron, acts as a neurotransmitter or chemical messenger to communicate with other neurons.

Cognitive bias: Noun; a systematic error in thinking that occurs when people are processing and interpreting information in the world around them and affects the decisions and judgments that they make.

Conduit: Noun; a channel for conveying water or other fluid or substances.

Contingency: Noun; a measure of co-variation between discrete events, condition where the presence and absence of event A predicts the presence and absence of event B.

Dopamine (DA): Noun; physiology, a chemical, produced by the neuron that acts as neurotransmitter or chemical messenger to communicate with other neurons; the neurotransmitter DA is utilized by cells of the ascending mesolimbic dopamine pathway, the brain's reward circuit.

Downregulation: Noun; neurobiology, the process of reducing or suppressing a response to a stimulus; the reduction in a cellular response to a molecule, chemical, or neurotransmitter, due to a decrease in the number of receptors on the cell surface.

Einstellung effect: Noun; Often called a problem solving set; a person's predisposition to solve a given problem in a specific manner even though better or more appropriate methods of solving the problem exist; a negative effect of previous experience when solving new problems.

Enigma: Noun; a person or thing that is mysterious, puzzling, inscrutable, or difficult to understand.

Etiology: Noun; medicine, the origins or genesis of, the cause or set of causes, or manner of causation of a disease or condition.

Euphoria: Noun; the emotional experience (or affect) of pleasure or excitement and intense feelings of well-being and happiness.

Heuristic: Noun; a process or method that enables a person to discover or learn something for themselves based on their personal experiences.

Illusion of control: Noun; the tendency for people to overestimate their ability to control events.

Incentive: Noun; a thing, such as a goal or payoff or reward, that motivates or encourages one to do something.

Instinct: Noun; an innate, typically hard-wired and pre-programmed fixed pattern of behavior in animals in response to certain stimuli.

Intravenous (iv): Adjective; medicine, route of administration of fluids or substances into the body, existing or taking place within, or administered into, a vein or veins.

Intuition: Noun; the ability to understand something immediately, without the need for conscious reasoning, informal knowledge or understanding.

Major depressive disorder (MDD): Noun; medicine, a mental health disorder characterized by persistently depressed mood or loss of interest in activities, causing significant impairment in daily life.

Melancholia: Noun; medicine, an extreme form of depression characterized by a deepened or prolonged sadness in everyday life, sustained inability to experience pleasure.

Midbrain: Noun; neuroanatomy, the midbrain or mesencephalon is the forward-most portion of the brainstem and is associated with basic and primitive survival functions, including vision, hearing, motor control, sleep and wakefulness, arousal (alertness), and temperature regulation.

Neophobia: Noun; fear of anything new, unwillingness to try new things or break from routine; reject the unknown or the novel.

Neurobiology: Noun; neuroscience, the study of cells of the nervous system and the organization of these cells into functional circuits that process information and mediate behavior; a subdiscipline of both biology and neuroscience.

Neurophysiology: Noun; a branch of physiology and neuroscience that is concerned with the study of the functioning of the nervous system.

Neuropsychiatry: Noun; medicine, a branch of medicine that deals with mental disorders attributable to diseases of the nervous system.

Neurotransmission: Noun; physiology, the transmission of nerve impulses between neurons (nerve cells of the brain or spinal cord) or between a neuron and a muscle fiber or other structure.

Neurotransmitter: Noun; physiology, a chemical substance that is released at the end of a nerve fiber by the arrival of a nerve impulse and, by diffusing across the synapse or junction, causes the transfer of the impulse to another nerve fiber, a muscle fiber, or some other structure.

Nociceptive reflex: Noun; physiology, withdrawal reflex (nociceptive flexion reflex or flexor withdrawal reflex) is a spinal reflex intended to protect the body from damaging stimuli.

Nucleus accumbens (NAC): Noun; neuroanatomy, part of the mesolimbic pathway, utilizes release of dopamine as neurotransmitter; often called the pleasure center or reward center of the brain.

Phenotype: Noun; genetics, the set of observable physical or behavioral characteristics of an individual resulting from the interaction of its genotype or genetic make-up with the environment.

Prefrontal cortex: Noun; neuroanatomy, the area of the cerebral cortex covering the front part of the frontal lobe, implicated in planning complex cognitive behavior, personality expression, decision making, and moderating social behavior.

Promissory note: Noun; a signed document containing a written promise to pay a stated sum to a specified person or the bearer at a specified date or on demand.

Psychological scotoma: Noun; a type of blind spot that occurs in the way we view reality. It means there is information in our experience that is inconvenient for our ego, and it responds by turning a 'blind eye' to it.

Psychomotor activation: Noun; pharmacology, a behavioral index of stimulant psychopharmacology characterized by augmented locomotion and stereotyped behaviors (stereotypy), derived primarily from activation of dopamine release.

Psychopathology: Noun; psychiatry, the scientific study of mental disorders.

Refractory: Adjective; medical, resistant to a process or a stimulus, stubborn or unmanageable, unresponsive, intractable.

Ritual: Noun; a religious or solemn ceremony consisting of a series of actions performed according to a prescribed order.

Salient: Adjective; most noticeable or important, prominent, conspicuous.

Sensitization: Noun; the quality or condition of responding to certain stimuli in a sensitive manner, the process of enhancing reactivity or responsiveness to a stimulus or condition.

Sign-tracking: Noun; Pavlovian conditioning of a behavior that is directed towards a stimulus due to a learned association between that stimulus and a reward. The sign-tracking response develops even though reward delivery is not contingent upon a response. Synonyms: Autoshaping; Pavlovian conditional approach.

Subliminal: Adjective; refers to a stimulus or a mental process below the threshold of sensation or consciousness; perceived by or affecting someone's mind without their being aware of it.

Topography: Noun; the description of the form or shape of a sequence of motor responses.

Ventral tegmentum (VTA): Noun; neuroanatomy, a cluster of neuronal cell bodies located close to the midline on the floor of the midbrain, ventral tegmental area (VTA) neurons utilize dopamine as neurotransmitter and project terminals to the nucleus accumbens, involved with reward and addiction.

WYSIATI: Noun; abbreviation or acronym for "What You See Is All There Is", formulated by Daniel Kahneman as one of the human biases that underlies decision-making that is not entirely based on rational thought.

Made in the USA
Middletown, DE
08 September 2020